Speaking From My Mind

Speaking From My Mind

Chukwuma Julius Okonkwo

Library of Congress Control Number:		2019907664
ISBN:	Hardcover	978-1-7960-4019-7
	Softcover	978-1-7960-4018-0
	eBook	978-1-7960-4017-3

Print information available on the last page.

Rev. date: 06/12/2019

To order additional copies of this book, contact:
Xlibris
1-888-795-4274
www.Xlibris.com
Orders@Xlibris.com
798381

CONTENTS

DEDICATION

In memory of Julius Nwankwo Ogomegbunam
Okonkwo and Onyebuchi Francis Okonkwo

PREFACE

ANYBODY WHO KNOWS me well might not be surprised that I wrote this book, but rather might be disappointed at me that it took me a long time to decide to write this book. Though, I have been writing for over a decade, however, I have never felt convinced to publish a book until the mid-2017. The urge to write fully started when I first had my name appear in a printed newspaper. Then a national daily newspaper in Nigeria (I think, This Day) had a section called 'constitutional conference' where political issues were discussed and public responses were welcomed. My short response to one of the topical issues was published and I felt really good to see my name printed on a national daily newspaper. At that time I had joined Facebook, so that stimulated my mind to use Facebook to publish in the form of notes the things that I wrote about.

In 2012, a friend asked me if I knew how to create a blog. Apparently, she wanted to start blogging. I did not know how to create a blog, but I took it as a challenge to figure it out. After I had created the blog for my friend, I thought it would be nice to create mine; at least I would stop publishing notes on Facebook. In September 2012, I started blogging. I was writing on a spectrum of things, for example, socio-economic, political and religious issues, as well as fiction and poetry. I felt comfortable with sharing my ideas on my blog. I did not realize how people valued what I was publishing on my blog until I stopped blogging for a while. The encouragement from a few family and friends to continue blogging was amazing. I realized that people were influenced in a positive way by the things that I blogged.

From publishing on my blog, I thought it would be great to publish articles on newspapers. So, I started writing to publish on news media – online and printed. At first, my submissions did not get published. I devised a simple approach, which was that if I submitted an article to a news media and it did not get published, I would publish it on my blog. None of the editors told me why they would not publish my articles, but I figured it out myself. I changed the way I write for a news media publication. Sometimes it worked and sometimes it did not. There is no magic bullet to it; it is all about the editor's perspective at that point in time. I was patient too, because I knew that as an inchoate writer there would be thorns on the path of getting published. So, patience and persistence were the garments that I wore all the time. Subsequently, the gate of acceptance opened and my submissions started receiving acceptance.

For me, writing is an avenue to share my views about certain phenomena and contribute to debates on topical issues happening within my country and around the world. I am mostly driven to write when I am bothered about an issue. I did not quite realize that my writings were making positive impacts on people until I started receiving messages on Facebook from friends, asking for my thoughts on certain topical issues within and outside my country. Some friends, and even strangers, have sought my advice on how they could start publishing articles, like I do, on national daily newspapers, because they were inspired by the things I wrote about and the way I wrote them. Indeed, those messages meant a lot to me and somewhat inspired me to write more, but time was never on my side. For those people, I hope this book will inspire you to work towards writing your own book. This brings me to the reason why I wrote this book.

I wrote this book for one reason. The reason is to share my thoughts on the things that deeply concern me, some of which I had written previously about and some were fresh thoughts based on my sobering experiences in and perceptions about life. The title of the book expressly makes this reason clear that it is about my thoughts, which I expect many people to challenge. I have always thought about life in a much deeper sense, with the hard times that I have faced in life, and I have realized that the lessons that I have learnt in my journey of life so far might give some people somewhere in the world insights into how to deal with their challenges in life or even change some aspects of their lives that hinder them from living the life of their dream. I have always wanted to write in ways that expose people to different sides to life and ways to think about life, because I am often concerned about the way certain concepts are obtusely conceptualized and interpreted, while some are deliberately ignored and not discussed to our danger and at the danger of our societies. So, in this book, I discussed issues that have moral bents, some of which readers may find unconventional, and some of which many people are not exposed to, or perhaps are exposed to but for some reasons they are somehow in denial and unwilling to discuss. There is no single way to make the world a better place. I think that we can make a difference in people's life through the things we write about and the ways we write about them. Life is about learning and sharing experience. This book is my own way of helping people to gain insights that can change their lives. The book provokes many thoughts for readers to think about.

Throughout the book I have tried to explore life and its challenges in different contexts with different stories and analogies. That to a large extent involved using some personal experiences and imaginary scenarios to drive home some points and provoke thoughts. I love to tell stories and this book is somehow a reflection of that love for story-telling, though not in a conventional way. Some imaginary stories were deliberately told to help readers understand better some concepts that they might or might not have been exposed to and the contexts of different discussions. Some of these stories may sound unconventional to readers; hence may upset their conventional views about some concepts and life in general. However, the objective of this book is not to portray conventional or popular ideas; rather it is to persuade readers' conviction to think about or see things differently. The aim is that by the end of this book, you will have been persuaded based on the scenarios that have been painted to think about life differently from your usual way of thinking and as such be able to challenge the things you think you already know. The book is about getting readers to think about life in different ways, it is about provoking thoughts, and it is about inspiring and motivating people. It is my way of speaking to people that I may not have the opportunity to speak to directly. In some cases, the ideas in the book may risk oversimplification, however, readers must keep in mind that the book is about my thoughts as influenced by my checkered and sobering experiences in life.

CHAPTER 1

Be Your Brother's Keeper

A S A CHILD born into a Christian home, one of things that fascinated me about Christianity was the scripture. I loved the way stories were told in the Bible. One of the scriptures that captured my imagination as a child was the story about Cain and Able in Genesis 4. But as I grew up, I began to learn from experiences that it is the business of man on earth to look after himself. It is often said that it is all man for himself. These are clichés often used to describe the world under the old ethics – when the ethics of life were based on the rule of the jungle; the ethics of the wild beast. Those were the old times; the eras of barbarism, and the old world; the uncivilized world. In that world, you would take care of yourself, no matter what might become of your fellow man. If you were asked the whereabouts of your fellow man, you would respond, like Cain in Genesis 4:9, that you were not your brother's keeper.

Though, we live in a modern world today, however, we still act like we are in the old world. We still ask that question Cain asked Jesus thousands of years ago: "Am I my brother's keeper?" Even when we try to put an answer to it our answers do not reflect the civilized world that we claim to live in today. Survival of the fittest has become our way of life. Survival has become the ultimate goal and the means of survival, the struggle. Complacency has become the watchword. Our comfort zone is what matters to us the most and we do not want to get out of that zone to do something for others. If something does not have anything to do with us, we do not get involved in it. If something is not our business, we do not show concern. We have become so attached to our own world that we do not realize that there are worlds outside of our own. Once we get in, we shut others out. We have been caught up in our own circle such that we often think that everything revolves around the cyclic way of life we have created for ourselves. We have become so engrossed in what is ours that we care less of the things that affect others and even the things that we do that affect them. All the time we want attention to be focused on us, regardless of what other people may be going through. We tend to see the world through a single lens and we want to direct the movement of that lens.

In my interactions with people, I have observed that our level of concern about the needs of other people has astronomically degenerated. This is because there is an increased attitude of 'I do not care' or 'what's my business with that' going on around the world. This attitude has caused systemic gangrene of the fabrics of many societies and communities. There is scarcity of real love because these days love has been commoditized. Love has a price tag now and it can be bought and sold. This is why there are often strings attached to love. We do not love our neighbours anymore as much as we love ourselves. We use others as litmus tests for what we cannot do unto ourselves. Our self-centric mentality has caused us to ignore the fact that we are surrounded by people who are in dire need of help. There are many people suffering from all kinds of mental health issues, like depression and suicide. Most times we do not even notice that people close to us have these issues, because we often overlook them. We overlook them because we focus so much on ourselves and our wants.

However, there is always a tipping point in everything. Now let me speak to some people. Imagine someone who is always around you, perhaps your loved one, is suffering from depression and you have no idea, because you are always concerned about yourself. Even when you see the signs that something may not be alright with the person you tend to ignore the signs. You fail to ask about the person's welfare, you fail to talk about the person's situations, and you fail to care about the person's needs. Then one day you receive the news that the person has taken the unconventional path to death – the person has committed suicide. Then you wonder why the person took his or her life. You even become judgemental because you cannot understand it.

Indeed, there are many challenges that people face in life that do not simply reveal themselves on the face. Sometimes we may see the signs and sometimes the signs are hidden under the surface of their smiles that we do not see them. You may know what someone is going through if you ask. Sometimes when you ask, the answers do not easily come out until you show that you care. I have been in many difficult situations in life where everything seemed like a cul-de-sac. Then I felt like I was in the wilderness where it was just me and my problems. There was the feeling that nobody would understand my situations, except me. So, I would decide to bottle up whatever I was facing, but never would I bottle out, because I always face my challenges. It would take someone who really cares, not by what s/he said to me, but by actions, for me to reveal what I was passing through. There are many people who are like me. People are not always sincere when it comes to helping others. When you observe that someone may be going through difficult times, you just have to show love and concern to find out what is eating them up.

Also, imagine a world where everything is just about you. Your slogan is all man for himself. If it is not your headache you cannot be bothered to buy panadol. Safety measures exist only when your security or privacy is breached. If there is no black out in your house you do not care whether the power is cut off in your neighbourhood. You always tell the story whenever you are the victim, but if you are not the victim the story is worthless. It is always about your perspective and opinion. When churches and mosques are attacked; you do nothing because you are an atheist. When LGBTQs (Lesbians, Gay, Bisexual, Transgender and Queer) are persecuted; you say nothing because you are straight. When women are violated and abused; you do nothing because you are a man. When children are abused and killed; you are not troubled because you have no child. When people of colour are racially discriminated against; you maintain your silence because you are white. If the issues affect the white people; you show no concerns because you are not white, so it is white people's problem. When people with disability are discriminated against; you do nothing because you do not have any disability. When waters and environments are polluted

SPEAKING FROM MY MIND

in communities; you do nothing because you live in a safely protected environment. When schools and institutions of higher learning are closed down; you maintain your silence because your children study overseas. When hospitals are dysfunctional and there is no access to healthcare; you do nothing because you have a private hospital or receive medical treatments overseas. When animals are brutally murdered; it is not your concern because you do not like animals.

Then one day your house is attacked, assassins have come knocking on your door; you call for help, but nobody answers because you have done nothing for others and you have been silent about other people's problems all your life. So, you receive the payment in your own coin. You are deserted, everyone becomes deaf to hear you calling, and you are faced with the evils that you have done staring you in the face. The seed that you sow today is what you will reap tomorrow. What you do for people today when they are in trouble will determine what they will do for you tomorrow when you are in trouble. It is always good to treat people nice today if you wish to be treated nice tomorrow. The person you gave the reason to live today might be the person that will save your life tomorrow. These are the undertones of the golden rule. The golden rule teaches us to treat others the same way we would want them to treat us. But, we often twist the golden rule. We want others to apply the golden rule to us, but we do not apply it to other people, because of our greed and selfishness.

But, we must understand that life is not about taking all the advantages to ourselves. We must develop the mind-set that we can only build a better and freer world for all by dedicating ourselves to the concept of being our brother's keeper. That should be the moral standard we must set to ourselves. It is a choice that we have to make. That choice is relevant because the challenges that people face these days are variegated. These challenges are not just about physical needs, but also about emotional needs. People go through lots of emotional pains, perhaps as a result of life threatening illness, or death of loved ones, or relationship issues, or career somersault. The pains arising from these challenges can be excruciating and the burdens can be overwhelming. But, because we are used to ignoring the physical needs of other people,

CHUKWUMA JULIUS OKONKWO

we do not notice these emotional needs. These needs come with feelings of helplessness, barrenness, desolation, and loneliness. These feelings can be irresistible. When you are in deep emotional pains there is often a subtle and overpowering voice that tells you to do some unimaginable things. At that point you need a companion who will show you love and care, who will pray for you, who will help you to activate your faith in yourself, who will help you to keep your eyes on what is at stake, and who will help you to restore your peace of mind. This is what we need to do for people around us and people we meet in our journey of life. We should allow our moral compass to direct our courage to always be our brother's keeper. By being our brother's keeper we will always care about other people's physical and emotional well-beings.

As we walk through this path called earth, let being our brother's keeper be the title that inspires us to live and love. Loving and caring for someone who is in physical or emotional need is like giving water to someone who is really dehydrated. Imagine the feeling and satisfaction when you drink a glass of (cold) water after a long period of thirst for water. That is a similar feeling and satisfaction that people who are in need of something get when we help them. Imagine the feeling and frustration when nobody can offer you a glass of water when you need water the most. People are thirsty for different things in life and people are hungry for different things. Being our brother's keeper helps us to notice those things that matter the most to people. Being our brother's keeper enables us to offer to other people the glass of water that can revive them and keep them alive. Being our brother's keeper requires us to show love and care to other people, to notice their needs and be concerned about those needs, and to be aware of the things that we do that may affect other people. Being our brother's keeper is simply looking after one another. Most times what people need the most are just love, care, friendship and prayers. These are not difficult to give. We should learn how to give them to the people who need them because that is the only way we can be our brother's keeper and above all make our societies and communities better and freer for all to live and love.

CHAPTER 2

Because They Are Women

WE LIVE IN a crazy world where strange things that cringe our minds happen. One of the craziest things that I have seen is how men pleasurably pass judgements on women like men are naturally ordained to do so. This tends to make women look inferior to men. The worst is that many societies are structured in ways that make this rampant. I grew up witnessing how women are stripped naked in public for allegedly committing crimes, like stealing a neighbour's yams or chickens, that men would commit but men would not get stripped naked in public the same way women were stripped. Repeatedly, we saw women arbitrarily stripped naked and offensively humiliated in public by a mob, mostly men. From the society getting accustomed to women getting stripped naked in public it progressed to people finding pleasure in spreading daguerreotyped nude pictures of women with the help of technology like the internet.

Today, it would appear to be normal for men, especially, to spread on the internet nude pictures of their female partners when the relationship is severed. Given the rampancy of such a despicable act, it would seem that the society has lost its head when it comes to issues like stripping a woman naked and parading her in public for an alleged crime. In the process of that act, people will take pictures of the woman's nudity and spread on social media, like Facebook and Twitter. These days there are many people who sit and wait for such an opportunity, once it happens they will jump on it and help in spreading those pictures in a speed of light. If you have seen any of those pictures I am sure they cringed your mind like they did to mine. There is no best way to describe the disgust, or quantify the mental irritations that come with such acts. They are really unthinkable.

CHUKWUMA JULIUS OKONKWO

Though, it is worrisome that such things happen, but what is more worrisome is that even women participate in the spreading spree of nude images of their fellow women. If it was on Facebook that such images were posted, the comments, particularly from women, that would follow the post would baffle you. It is worrisome that some women do not see the gender stereotypes that are associated with those contemptible acts. When women do not show concern about serious gender issues that should concern them, then men will be inspired to take pleasure in exposing women's nudity. Sometimes I deliberately try to join issues with some women to get a sense of why some women are blind to see the gender insensitivity in those acts. It surprises me that the premise of their argument is often judgmental; they cast blames on the victims. For the woman who was stripped naked in public for allegedly stealing her neighbour's chickens, the blame is often why she stole in the first place; after all it is not in the character of a woman to steal. For the woman whose male partner exposed her nude picture on the internet, the blame is often that it serves her right; after all she should have been smarter than sending her nude photos to a man. To say that those comments coming from women were shocking would verge on simplicity. Unfortunately, that is the reality of the world we live in today. Many women are blind to see the serious gender issues that characterize those acts and as such they lack the energy to engage in discussions to put an end to those acts.

Many times I have heard the saying that it is a man's world. You may have heard that many times too. In fact, it has become a cliché. But, is the world really a man's world? If you think about that saying deeply you will understand why many societies are deeply rooted in patriarchy, and why societal dispositions in many societies oppose strongly the principle of equality of gender and scorn women very much. At the heart of that cliché is the gender insensitivity that has characterized the world today. Majority of women have succumbed to the discriminating concepts behind that cliché. One of such concepts is male dominance. Some people have argued that the notion of male dominance started from the time God created man and woman, with God using Adam's rib to create Eve. But I am not persuaded by that notion. I do not see the relevance of the divinity of creating a woman out of a man's rib to the dominance of a man over a woman. Unfortunately, this notion has inundated many thinking across the world. For me, one thing is that God created Eve out of Adam's rib, and another thing is that God did not decree that Adam was to be dominant over Eve. It is, therefore, the (mis)interpretation that has been given to the divine creation of man and woman that has misinformed the dominance of men over women. Even if by a stretch of the imagination that God upon creating Adam and Eve decreed that Adam was to be dominant over Eve, should the dominance of Adam over Eve be interpreted as dehumanization of Adam over Eve, especially in the contexts of increased discrimination against women in all forms that we see today?

Many times I have tried to understand why the act of sharing a woman's nudity on the internet has become pleasurable. Each time I try I end up provoking more questions than I could provide answers to. It is often easier to ask questions than provide answers. I have tried to formulate a proposition that somehow helped me to understand the concept behind those acts. This proposition centers on the opposite of the usual 'why' question. Often times if you want to understand something the usual question to ask is why. Let us imagine why a man would expose to the public the naked pictures of a woman, shared in confidence with him, perhaps when she was overly in love. Let us ask why a woman would be stripped completely naked for allegedly committing a crime? Why do our societal practices still oppose strongly the principles of gender equality? Why do we hardly see male armed robbers stripped completely naked the same way women are stripped in the part of the world where stripping a woman naked is rampant? Why do people spread those pictures? Why do women take part in the spreading spree, rather than repudiating in strong terms those acts? We cannot pose enough many 'why' questions. The answer to these why questions lies in the opposite, 'why not.' If you attach 'not' to each of the 'why' questions posed above or any 'why' question that you provoke yourself, you will see the answers come out smoothly and stare you in the face. It is simply because they are women. If not why would the acts happen in the first place?

CHUKWUMA JULIUS OKONKWO

The premise upon which gender stereotype against women is formed is simply 'why not', which is followed by the reason that they are women. Many times I have heard women being described as the weaker sex, created out of the abundance of men, and as such they should be eternally inferior for such a divine gesture. I cannot express enough in words how untrue such an ignorant description is and how I detest such a misguided description. If you asked a guy why he would comfortably expose on the internet her girlfriend's nude pictures, perhaps as retaliation for something, you would hear something like, why not, she is a woman. If you asked an angry mob that stripped a woman completely naked for allegedly stealing her neighbour's chickens, the response would not be far from why not, she is a woman. I, therefore, would argue that those acts take place by the simple fact that the victims are women. Men perceive women as inferior to them, so they always try to live out that mind-set. If not, how many women have we seen expose their male partner's nude pictures on the internet? You think women are not in possession of those kinds of pictures from their male partners? It shows the difference between the character of men and women. Though we tend to see women as the weaker sex, but in reality men's actions often reveal men as the weaker sex. Men often think that superiority of sex lies in their display of masculine muscular endowments. I admire the most the ability of women to maintain resilience in the face of trials and tribulations. For me that conquers any masculine muscular showcase.

Moreover, the logic behind 'why not' appears to be more dominant than 'why'. This means that if you are looking for a reason to do something or justify your actions, asking yourself 'why' will not be as convincing as asking 'why not'. For example, if you want to punish somebody, you would rather ask 'why should you not punish the person' than ask 'why you should punish the person'. If you were considering playing hooky, perhaps from work or school, asking yourself 'why you should play hooky' would not give you the convincing reason to play hooky, but asking 'why should you not' play hooky would provide you with the needed reasons to play hooky. Also, a child who wanted to stay awake at night beyond his or her bed time, perhaps to play a little bit more would be more interested in asking his or her parents why s/he would not be allowed more time to play than if she would be allowed more time to play. What I have demonstrated here is that the logic behind 'why not' tends to outshine the logic behind 'why'; hence making 'why' some sort of sterilized version of 'why not'. Perhaps if the people who have found pleasure in exposing or sharing women's nudity ask themselves why they are doing it they might not be persuaded to do it, so they prefer the easier option, which is why will they not do it, and that provides them the reason to do it.

In the world that we live in today, privacy is seen as a privilege to women. With all the civilization and modernization in the world, some men still believe strongly that a woman has no privacy because she is seen as a property that is acquired and owned by a man; hence her privacy is in a man's palm. The fact that such thinking exists in 21st century is rather appalling. It should worry us, and as such we must desist from such thinking. This thinking is driven by the notion of male dominance, which has become ingrained in many societies and as such has become recalcitrant. Male dominance is manifested in public and private sector institutions, where serious gender issues are given less attention. We see the imprints of male dominance in glass ceilings in various aspects of life. There is so much dehumanization of women going on around the world today; the insensitivity of society to women issues is on the rise, and the silence of the judicial system to the high spate of gender stereotypes and discriminations against women echoes loudly in many countries. These are all manifesting simply because the people we should ordinary be taken as our equal are women. Therefore, because they are women they are less human beings than men, is that right? No it is not!

CHAPTER 3

Building African Literary Writing

ONE CAN EASILY count the number of African literary writers who make a living from their written works. When you look at the number of people, who have become interested in African writing as a profession or investing in African literary works, it is disappointing, in my opinion. This suggests that if progressive changes are not urgently made to change this disappointing situation, the future of African literary writing will be nothing to write home about. We should be worried about this and as such must do something to change it. I have listened to international award winning African literary writers talk about African literary writing and they are often ambiguous in their responses to whether an African writer needs to leave African soil for Europe or America before s/he can get published or win a literary award. I have listened to literary veterans talk about the ridiculous experiences that they went through before their works saw the limelight. It is worrisome that after many decades young aspiring generation of writers still face, today, the same challenges that the older generation faced in those old times. I understand quite well and believe without doubts that there are some inevitable challenges a young aspiring writer has to grapple with at the start of his or her writing career. But, I do not believe that we should keep recycling this enduring myth that an African writer cannot get published within the four walls of his or her country or Africa and still gain international recognition without fleeing abroad for such purposes. This myth and its associated syndrome is the parent of other problems faced by African literary writing. To be clear, there is nothing wrong if an African writer chooses to be published overseas. But, there is something fundamentally wrong if it becomes a quest that is pursued based on the notion that what is outside is better than what we have inside. There is everything wrong if it is established as a contour of the African writing.

Take a look at the marginalized African literature. We have lost gravity on African perspectives in our quest to get published abroad. The way African stories are told has been twisted to reflect the mainstream views that sell easily in the West. As a result, Africans have spent decades invigorating the perspectives of the western writings, thus pushing to the abyss of history the untapped historical stories of Africa. This is why we read unending horrible stories being told about Africa and its people. It is for that same reason that we see images of our beautiful and charming young girls offensively daguerreotyped with their nudity and arbitrarily exposed in the name of portraying the culture of Africa and telling a story of how we lived or live in Africa. We, Africans, are accomplice. By posting and/or sharing on social media, for example Facebook or Twitter, we help to fuel those obnoxious and human degrading images. We provide the platform that inspires the kind of absurd comments that follow those images. Also, because we have left our stories in the hands of foreigners, images of our children occupy their web pages and form the front page of their charity campaign programmes. You only see images of our children on CNN (Cable Network News), BBC (British Broadcasting Corporation) and the likes, only when the topic of discussion is poverty or hunger or some sort of endemic disease. But, when they talk about inventions and innovations by young people, African children and youths are not worthy to be featured; rather Western children and youths are worthy choices. Even the donor agencies that claim to be champions of causes against poverty and hunger are culprits. When they are fundraising for projects or programmes that target poverty and hunger, images of our loving mothers and children are used to make emotional appeals. What a strategic way to remind us that our continent is full of children dying of diseases, hunger and poverty. But, they do not tell the stories of our children achieving impressive feats in STEM (science, technology, engineering and mathematics) because that would seem counterproductive to their campaigns.

Take a look at the perspectives of African publishers (or publishing companies). They fuel this long-lasting myth and syndrome by giving attention to only literary works they perceive as lucrative and capable of bringing home literary prizes. Basically, they prefer to count the chickens before they are hatched. Their minds are so fixed on the lucrative side of literary writing that they push young writers to write stories that paint neatly conjured images of the West and leave our own stories untold at the mercy of foreign writers, who often lack the deep understanding and real knowledge of who we are as Africans. This is why you see American writers telling us our stories based on what they read from the map, and European writers writing about Africa based on what their data reveals to them, and sometimes after the data had been flogged to speak in consonant with their a priori assumptions. It is worrisome how often we value what comes from the outside over what we have within. I am sometimes tempted to wonder if this is a sign of loss of purpose or sheer ignorance. This is what happens when writing and publishing is viewed from the lens of profitmaking. We must redress our steps and redefine our purpose for writing and publishing because the drive for profitmaking is tearing our African literary writing house apart. We must not let this house to collapse!

Take a look at the fallout of this quest for international recognition. It has tied our culture of writing to imitating the existing writers with endearing international bents. We have lost our originality as we strive to write like the Americans and the Europeans, who will never wish to write like us. We are often tempted to substitute in our poetry our African poetic surrealism to a western imagination. I must confess that sometimes I fall a victim of that too. I guess we are often tempted to show the level of our exposure to the Western knowledge. Then we risk substituting what should be African perspective with a foreign perspective. In doing that we fail to understand that our cultural and structural heterogeneity, that is those characteristics that make us different, cannot be juxtaposed with the ones that are alien to us. We are often glued to the Western ideology that we lose focus of what is happening in our immediate environment. The resultant effect is that we have become acculturated. If the writing does not have international bent it is not convincing. By internalizing Western ways of writing we make a big deal out of the things that are external to us rather than the things that are internal.

Every continent has its own way, I believe. Like the Europeans have the European way or Americans have the American way, we have our African way. This is an idea we must proclaim. But how can we proclaim what we often do not notice? We lose sight of the things that make us unique as Africans. Because we do not notice those things we do not write about them. Because we do not write about them nobody knows about them. They are lost in history. Our dynamic self-possession and self-determination are our personal charms that make us different. With our charms we can change these surviving myth and syndrome that make us think that we cannot succeed unless we pass through the liberality and benevolence of the Western liberators, who pose as saviour to us.

Though our challenges as African literary writers are many, however, they are not insurmountable. The era of African literary writing is fast taking twist positive turns. Many African literary writers are taking massive and unrelenting efforts to portray our lost-and-found and unheard stories. Young African literary writers are inspired by the success stories of successful African writers, who made it to the limelight from within Africa, and are encouraged to not just write but expose in their writings the wrong impressions portrayed about Africa. The wind of change has drastically begun to blow across African literary writing. Publishers have also woken up from their slumber to embrace the challenges facing African literary writing. All we need is sustainability. But, we can only sustain the progressive changes that have been made across Africa by keeping African literary writing alive at all times. We must not let this burning fire to be extinguished. When I interact with young Africans I see the passion and resilience in them. I see young people who are poised to change the continent with their positive energy. I hear their success stories sounding loud like a trumpeting elephant in the forest.

Look at the South, East, North and West Africa; see how writers have repositioned themselves to overcome the challenges of writing we are facing. Africa is now posed by the West as a holy grail. This is because there is something we possess that is valuable to them. They cannot get their eyes off it. But, we cannot lose it to them too. We are progressing and shall not fail to question or correct any prevailing notion that is not in tandem with our heritage. It is our story and we must tell it our own way, the way it will make sense to our generation and generations to come. We are not here to impress the outsiders. That is not my purpose on earth. And that should not be your purpose too.

Indeed, the syndrome of African aberrance and inferiority complex will soon be eroded from our minds. Though changing these myths and syndromes is not an easy task, as they are recalcitrant and do not die easily, however confidence is important. Resilience is the watchword. Rather than uploading and sharing obscene daguerreotypes of our naked young girls for the pleasure of those unrepentant paedophiles, or images of our poor children, dressed in threadbare and tattered clothes and unkempt hairs, posing barefooted, we can change the story by juxtaposing those pictures with scenic images of the same young girls wearing our glamorous and eye-catching traditional wears, showing their elegance, the same children wearing unspoiled and well-dressed clothes, showing their pristine nature, and the same children breaking records in STEM, posing with their inventions. Those images and ugly stories behind them represent the perceptions, which do not reflect who we are and what we aspire to become. We must see them as barriers that must be broken; otherwise we may become comfortable with them and not be inspired to deal with them. By that we would be sending across to the world the idea that women whose nudity were daguerreotyped abysmally, now alluring, and children whose images were shabbily portrayed as poverty-stricken, now healthy and nourishing, are worthy of respect like their Western counterparts.

The older generation of patriotic African writers has set the pace for us, the younger generation. We have to take up the baton and keep the ball rolling. But, the kind of baton we pass on to the next generation depends on the steps we take today. My message is simple: live like an African; tell the story of Africa like an African; help to rebuild Africa; and hope to die an African, which you were born.

CHAPTER 4

Compartment of Life

THERE IS NO single way to life. Life has been described in many ways. Sometimes it is described as a mystery. It is hard to understand life in its full essence. I have spent a considerable amount of time thinking about life. No matter how hard I try to understand life in its full essence there are always pieces of puzzles to assemble. So, I end up losing my mind all the time. But, life is full of fun in shades of colour; hence it should be lived to the fullest. That is one of my guiding philosophies in life. Most times when we look at ourselves in the mirror we easily notice how much we have grown physically, and we pay much attention to our physical appearance. But, less do we notice or pay attention to what goes beyond our physical appearance. We oftentimes fail, unconsciously, to notice how much we have grown or failed to grow inwardly as human beings. It will not be illogical to say that our outward appearance has taken preference over our inward appearance. Thus our inward life now exists as a sterilized version of the life we live on the outside.

I live life the way good conscience tells me is the best for me. I live by presumption of faith. By that I see my faith as my guiding light. I see my faith in myself as the cornerstone of my success. I see my faith in God as the foundation of my existence. I see my faith in people as the keystone that sustains my relationships. I have met a lot people in my little journey so far on earth, with different characters. I have seen that there are many people who live their lives for others. When you see them they look good on the outside, but on the inside they are devastated. They may own their physical bodies but the key to their inner selves is in the hand of other people, perhaps their families or friends.

CHUKWUMA JULIUS OKONKWO

Today, a lot of people live a life of validation. This means that they want to be accepted by everybody, so they cannot live without seeking other people's approval or opinion about their lives or situations. They have sabotaged their dreams by seeking validation. Sometimes most people see validation as being deferential. But, there is a huge gap between deference and validation. It is the former when you are in control of your emotions, you still have access to your emotions, and you know when and when not to seek opinions or advice. However, it is the latter when you have lost control of your emotions, you have given your emotional access to other people, and you cannot think without asking others what and how you should think. With a life of validation, a lot of people live in other people's pocket, where they see the world, not through their own lens, but the lens worn by other people.

Indeed, a life of validation should worry us. Many people are caught up in this life. You may have seen them, or you may be one of them. You cannot move forward if you always depend on other people to tell you what to do before you do them. You cannot live that successful life you always dream about if you cannot make a decision without waiting for someone to validate it. You are bound to live an unfulfilled life if you subject yourself to a low position where other people's opinions about your life are superior to yours. A life of validation has many off-springs. It is the reason why people disrespect you and have no regards for you. At the heart of such a life is sycophancy, and we are often persuaded by that sycophancy. We should be worried by the insincerity and futility that such sycophancy portrays. With such a life your happiness dangles in the palms of other people and they play with your emotions however they want, like toys.

Now let me speak to some people. You may be amongst the people who twist the image of themselves in order to fit into other people's mosaic, because you cannot paint your own canvas. You may be amongst people who lack the mind of their own and strive to satisfy everyone, while you are emotionally harried. You may be amongst people who buckle under other people's tension to change who they are, not because it is desirable for you to change, but because it satisfies what others want. You may be amongst people who lose the unique molds that make them who they are just to fit into other people's model. The danger of your life of validation is that you are sabotaging yourself and your future. As a result, you will end up becoming that clay that a mere skosh of water topples. You will become a fickle image in other people's tapestry of paintings. Hence you are remembered whenever you are needed; once you have finished what you are needed for you are forgotten until next period that necessity brings the need for you. To other people you are nothing but a tissue; you are used and dumped. That is how bad a life of validation can destroy someone.

Frankly, you do not need a life of validation to associate with other people. If you understand that you hold the master key to your life, which you should not under any circumstance hand over to someone else, then you will understand how demeaning a life of validation is. You do not need to give anyone that master key to your emotions for them to accept you. You do not have to blend with everybody for you to display how gregarious you are. You really do not need to live your life in someone's pocket because you want to be accepted by everybody. If people do not accept you for who you are, then they do not deserve you and you should not surround yourself with such people. If people – it does not matter who they are, your husband or wife, or your father or mother, or your uncle or aunty, or your siblings, or your boss or friends – do not respect you and you still stick around them, you only have one reason for that. That is because you do not value your worth. When you do not value your worth people will think you are worthless. Indeed, you do not need everyone around you to live a happy life. You only need few people who value and respect you.

Few years ago I had a friend who was going through crisis of a life of validation. Sometimes this may be inherited, like in my friend's case, and sometimes it may be a phase that we have to go through, perhaps to get what we want at certain point in our life. If the former is the case, then you have to break that cycle otherwise you will allow such a hereditary disaster to continue to infest your family lineage. The solution to a life of validation is placing your life into compartments and that is called compartment of life. This is a philosophy that I have imbibed and applied for years to my life. It has become my life guide.

CHUKWUMA JULIUS OKONKWO

It has helped me in my life's struggles and challenges. It has enabled me to know who and what deserves a place in my life. It has helped me to discover where I belong in other people's life too. It has helped me to be in charge of my emotions and my life, in general. It has helped me, most importantly, to be a better person.

When I told my friend that he needed to place his life into compartments he was flabbergasted because he did not understand what I meant. When I explained to him what he needed to do and how he would do it, it sounded like a crazy idea to him, initially, but when he understood the concept and applied it, his life was better off. It is a personal decision you can make for yourself, because it is according to your viewpoint. It is informed by the complexities of trying to cope with every person you meet in life. It is a coping mechanism. It is a refutation of highfalutin rules of validation of life that has enslaved many people. It will only work for you if you believe and put words into actions. But it, certainly, does not endorse separatism; it recognizes the primacy of the inseparable spiritual rule of life that advocates for togetherness of families and friends; and it validates the necessity of living a fulfilling life. Compartment of life is not persuaded by the notion that life should not be lived in compartments or the rhetoric of interpersonal relationships. You can place your life into compartments and still live a whole life and maintain healthy relationships with other people. It believes in the notion that not everybody or everything can fit into your life, that everybody or things should have distinct places in your life, and that you cannot fit into everybody's life too.

To understand this concept, let us assume that life is a single room. Obviously, the room cannot contain everything. We partition the room to create several places to put things in order. Without such a partition disorder is most likely to happen, as objects will be littered haphazardly. Imagine your clothes are placed in the kitchenette? Imagine your kitchen wares are placed on your futon? Imagine your dishes are placed in the lavatory? Imagine your toiletries are placed in the refrigerator? Imagine your shoes are placed on your lounger? It is a total mess, isn't it? Things need to be placed in their ideal places. With such a partition complementary objects, that is objects that complement themselves, are placed in the same place, while opposing objects, that is objects that cannot mingle, are placed in a different place. Such a partition makes every object in the room fall in where they belong, and the room quite habitable. Now you can picture your life in these two scenarios, with and without partition. Apply this concept to your life and let the single room signify your life. You can imagine how chaotic your life will be (or has been) in the first scenario, where there is no order and everything is littered. Imagine how peaceful your life will be in the second scenario, where everything is placed in the right places where they belong. We must always make a choice about the people we accept into our lives and surround ourselves with. Most times our brain is wired to the illusion that we have to fit into other people's life and fit ourselves into theirs. No we do not. We only have to fit them into ourselves where they rightly belong. If they do not fit in at all, then we let them go. That makes life simple.

Indeed, life is multifaceted. It is hard to blend with everybody or all the people you love. It is just impossible. You are better off dividing your life into different compartments, giving each person a specific compartment in your life and assigning values to each person. You assign values based on the magnitude of the compartments you reserve for them. This is perception against reality. Perception does not always reflect reality. It is always better to go with reality than perception because perception can be deceptive. When you compartmentalize your life you will not have to give much space to those who deserve little and vice versa; you will not have to give emotional access to your life to others who treat you less of a human being; and you will not need to feed anybody's personality to get accepted. You simply live your life the way you want to and most importantly be happy.

Compartment of life may not seem like a piece of cake, but it, certainly, can be quite easy if it is well-thought-out. The essence of compartment of life is to reduce your relationship confusions – with families or friends – and to install orderliness in your life. It does not suggest hate; rather it means you are letting people go. It means you are appropriately placing people where they belong. Even in the corporate world, organizations have different types of employees, for example workplace warriors, management mavericks, intrapreneurs, and entrepreneurs, each with its attendant values. They do not all get along. They understand and respect their boundaries. Thus compartment of life is for your own comfort level. It gives you the unusual power to take control of your life. It reminds you all the time that you are the captain of your life, that you hold the master key to your life and emotions, and that you have the power of choice to make your life look however you want it to look. You are a single soul, so you cannot accommodate everybody in your life and you cannot always fit into their lives no matter how you try to seek their validation. You must take control of yourself and your time with compartment of life. You will be marvelled at how transformed your life will become. Happiness is the key to life. Compartment of life will not only make your life simple, but will also help you to live a happy and fulfilling life.

CHAPTER 5

Excuses: Sweet Drugs That Kill Motivation

TAKE A LOOK at the dictionary meaning of the word excuse. You will find different contexts in which you can use the word. What I find from the different meanings of excuse and different contexts of its usage is that words, like reason or cause and outside are central to those meanings and contexts. This tells me that if you are giving excuses you are giving a reason or causing to be outside of something – it could be situations or circumstances, or actions or inactions, or conditions or phenomena. This suggests that you are not taking responsibility and by that you are giving up a cause or reason to take actions. Therefore, excuse is the reason to be outside a cause of action. It is a cause for no action, it tells you not to do what you are supposed to do, it teaches you not to take responsibility for your actions or inactions, and it deprives you the opportunity to take control of your life.

For me, excuses are sweet drugs that kill motivation. I have not seen anybody who is motivated by excuses. Taking responsibility motivates you, but giving excuses does not. I have seen people who often use their dysfunctional childhood experiences as excuses for the miserable life they are living. I have also seen people who use their adult life experiences as excuses for not accomplishing their goals in life. It is easier to blame somebody for your obstacles in life than it is to face your challenges. It is easy for younger generation to pass on to the older generation the blames for all the hardships in the economy. It is easy for children to blame their parents for the hunger and poverty in the family. It is easy for students to blame their teachers for failing examinations. It

CHUKWUMA JULIUS OKONKWO

is easy for graduates to blame the government if they cannot find jobs. It is easy for team members to blame the team leader for the team's failure. Giving excuses may be easy, but excuses, certainly, do not solve problems, they rather kill your motivation to provide answers to your questions or solutions to your problems. You are always giving excuses because you are unable to take responsibility. Excuses instil in your mind the fear of taking responsibility, which often prevents you from taking bold steps that can potentially change your life for good. That is why you always end up running around with your excuses soliciting for people's sympathy.

Most times it is easier to give excuses than to be responsible for your actions; hence you do not realize how much you are killing the stimulants in your brain that ordinarily gear you into taking the right steps to better your life. What you do not know is that each time you give excuses you are like a child that is lazy to toddle. Rather than the child to toddle, like every other child, s/he would remain on the ground waiting for someone to come and carry him or her. Your excuses do nothing but only encourage you to stick your lazy butt on the ground, like the child, while others are busy grinding to the hilt. When you tell people those pathetic stories about your life – how your parent(s) abandoned you when you were a child, how your families refused to help you with money for your education or business, how your friends always mock you because of your poor background, how your husband or wife maltreats you, or how every girl or boy you have dated always dumps you by sending you a break up text message. Obviously, people would feel sorry for you, and that would make you feel cool, right? But no amount of sorry from people will put you on the path of living the great life you always dream of. When you allow your excuses to deprive you the opportunity to make things right by being responsible for your actions or inactions, you are going off the path to your destiny, and no amount of sorry will put you back on the track you went off.

Therefore, you have got to activate your sense of purpose. You have to stop giving excuses, but accept the reason for your actions and be the cause of your actions. These are two different things. While the former means taking responsibility for your situation or what has happened, the latter means putting in hard work to make things right. I have seen friends who are accustomed to receiving hand-outs from family members or friends because of their bad situations. They have turned themselves into chronic recipients of alms. If no one gives them anything they mope about it. Second Corinthians 9:7 has become their favourite verse in the Bible. Please do not turn yourself into these people. That kind of life should worry you. If you have found yourself in that situation, please activate your sense of purpose in life. I have not seen anyone who gets rich by living off hand-outs. You cannot live that great life that you always dream of by living off charitable allowances. The excuses you give to make people feel sorry for you only make you an object of pity, and can only fetch you what I call pity packs – those (little) packages you receive from people when you indulge in self-pity. They are little because they cannot solve your problems, they can only alleviate your problems, which is like pushing the evil of today to tomorrow. Tomorrow your problems will come knocking on your door, your pity packs will have finished then, and you will be back to your story-telling, again. You have a choice to make, and that is to stop giving excuses that make you an object of pity.

Have you bothered to ask why people give excuses? It is because excuses are appealing. They appeal to you because you make them up. Your life experience is not an indication of what you are destined to become in life. Those childhood or adult life experiences that you always refer to when you look for sympathy are your past. You must leave the past where it belongs and embrace the future. You cannot allow your past to obstruct your future. Each time you invoke those stories to make people feel sorry for you and give you some pity packs you are torturing your future. Dwelling so much on your past will not lead you to your future destination. Life is a journey and there are challenges on the way. If you are always looking back to see what is behind you, you are wasting your time and you will never reach your destination in time. But, if you focus on what is in the front you will not only move faster, but will also reach your destination in time. This scenario paints a picture of what happens when you always dwell on your past. We have choices to make about our future and not about our past because we

CHUKWUMA JULIUS OKONKWO

can only control what is yet to happen and not what has happened. The choices you make determine the outcome of your life. Your childhood or adult life experiences should not be the judge of your present or future reality. You have the power of choice in your hands to re-write whatever story those bad experiences have written for you. What matters the most is not the situation you were born into, but what you do to get yourself out of that situation. I have seen people who were born with all kinds of disability, they did not allow their disability to define the outcome of their lives, but rather they used their disability as an ability to change their lives. Indeed, life will always present you with difficult challenges, but what you cannot do is to accept defeat. Life will always bring experiences that make it hard to live, but in your hand lies the choices to overcome your challenges.

If you have never been tested you will never know how good or bad you really are. Life would not be inspiring if everything was easy. We celebrate because we faced trials and tribulations and came out victorious. Trials and tribulations are great teachers you will ever learn from. Going through the storm makes you appreciate sunshine better when you finally see it at the end of the storm. The bitterness of famine creates the state of abundance, meaning that out of your struggles come success stories, but you have to put in hard work. If life was a bed full of roses we would all want to lay on it all day. Embracing our challenges teaches us how to deal with our demons – troubles that torment us – when they come knocking on our door. You would not learn to face your demons if none had ever confronted you. If you have never experienced pain you will think that it is easy to smile. If you have always had a smiling face you will not understand what having a frowned face looks like. The rain brings sunshine. There would not have been a sunny day if there was no rainy day. You would not know what joy feels like if you did not go through the pains. So when life brings you rains and pains, you have got to paddle through the rains and mellow amid your pains because you know that the rains will bring sunshine that will dry up the tragedies of raindrops in your life and the pains will bring joy that will sterilize your sorrowful times. Remember that success is achieved from the work done and not from the work to be done. This means that you have to put in hard work to change any situation that you do not like into something that you like. Sometimes your hard work may not pay off immediately because some things take time. But, it will surely pay off someday, perhaps when you do not even expect it. So, stop living in self-pity, stop complaining, stop making excuses, and be responsible for your actions. You must keep your faith alive. If your faith dies, your life becomes like a banana leaf that cannot wrap small pieces of cola nut.

Have you heard about point of reference (PoR)? Everybody has a PoR. This is something that you refer to for clarity when life gets tough. Your PoR is meant to be your life's guide. PoR is something personal to you; it can be a success story of what you have been through in life. That encourages you to strive for more success and to inspire others. Thus every time you face a challenge, you invoke the image of how you have succeeded in your previous challenges, and that fortifies you. Your PoR gives you extra energy to keep pushing. Excuses are boring PoR for life. Some people make excuses of why they are unsuccessful in life their PoR. How does that sound? This is when you live in self-pity and entertain people with your pity tales. How disappointing can it be that the things that you point to when life gets tough are your miserable experiences? Nobody is inspired by listening to excuses. People will be interested in how you turn the chaos in your life into a dancing star, and not in your pity tales. Your PoR is an integral part of who you become. When you dwell on dysfunctional experience of your childhood or the misery your adult life has exposed you to, you are simply giving your ugly life experiences the mandate to determine the outcome of your life. You have the power of choice to break away from any dysfunctional circumstances you have been through in life. When you make the same excuses your parents gave you for not becoming what they aspired to become, perhaps those are your parents' PoR, then you are simply recycling at your peril your parents' boring PoR. You do not need to replicate someone's version of PoR with your excuses. You need to create a blueprint of yourself for your success. So, stop making excuses that only give you a boring PoR.

Making excuses will not take you to the next level in your life. Excuses will always blind your sight for success. Excuses will always give you the wrong PoR. Excuses will always kill your motivational spirit and as such your goals die. Excuses are recipes for procrastination. While procrastination provides the first-class ticket to failure, excuses provide the incentives to procrastinate and give leverage to procrastination. There is nothing you have experienced or you are experiencing that somebody somewhere has not been through before. Resolve to change the experiences you have been exposed to, if they do not give you good PoR. Stop telling pity tales in order to receive pity packs. Adapt to the current reality of your life. If adaptation proves hard, motivate yourself with the hardest things you have accomplished before, let those things be your PoR. Excuses do not make histories. You cannot make a mark in the sand of time with your pity tales. But, you can leave that indelible mark, only with your actions guided by your right choices and reflected in hard work.

CHAPTER 6

Faith vs. Fate

I MAGINE YOU are offered a position, which requires executing a crucial project. This is the first assignment for anyone who assumes that position. The success or failure of this project will have a serious impact on your career. You do not have all the resources – financial, human and other resources – that you need to execute this project. You are told that there is no one who has held that position that has succeeded in executing the project. It is a difficult project and it can make or damage, not just your career, but also you as a whole. All the people – your family and friends – that you have discussed your intention to accept the position have advised you to decline the offer because they fear that you will fail and that will devastate you. That is something they do not want to see happen to you. The project is a Trojan horse; it sounds ambitious and achievable, but it was deliberately designed to fail, and that is why nobody has ever succeeded in executing it.

However, you accepted the offer and the challenge of executing the project, despite all the admonitions from your family and friends. Nobody can understand why you made that decision, but only you. Your decision is not based on any factual evidence, but your belief in yourself that you can successfully execute the project despite all odds. Deep down your heart, you do not know how you are going to do it with limited resources, but something within you strongly persuades your conviction that you can do it. That conviction is not based on the fact that you have never failed in your life, otherwise the fear of breaking your success records could have persuaded you to decline the offer. This is called faith. You made that decision based on presumption of faith. It does not matter whether you are a theist or an atheist. If you are a theist, your decision may have been informed by your faith in your God or god. That faith makes you believe that your God or god has guided you all your life to your successes and has never failed you. That faith made you to strongly believe that you can successfully execute that project. But, as an atheist, it is your faith in yourself that informed your decision.

Moreover, now you have accepted the offer and you are faced with the challenges of executing the project, your success or failure depends on the things that you have no control over. Your faith may have led you to accept the offer, but it may not lead you to a successful or unsuccessful outcome. Your fate decides the outcome. If it is your fate to succeed you will definitely succeed, if it is not, no matter how hard you try, you will fail. Thus, fate is something that is inevitable, it is something that if it is meant to happen it will surely happen and if it is not meant to happen it will surely not happen. So, you can see fate as a destiny that you cannot alter. Your faith tells you that you can successfully execute that project and it puts you in the direction to succeed. But, your fate decides whether you will succeed or not. Now you see that there is a stack distinction between faith and fate. However, there is a connection. Your faith can lead you to your fate. It is really hard to understand fate – how things are destined to happen and why they are destined. This is why fate is an abstract concept. And faith too is an abstract concept.

As abstract concepts, we cannot have an absolute understanding of faith and fate, or even the connection between them. In life there are many things that are beyond our power of understanding and reasoning, but based on our faith we still believe (in) them. I remember when I was a kid that my father used to throw me up in the air and catch me. I loved that playful act a lot. Sometimes I would spread my hands in the air like a bird while falling down into his hands and both of our faces would brim with smiles. That I felt comfortable descending from the air, with a face brimming with smiles, each time my father threw me up in the air was not just because I had faith in my father, but also because I trusted him. That trust made me to believe that he would never let me fall on the ground to injure myself. If I did not have that trust in my father I would not let him throw me up in the air. Thus, in the connection between faith and fate trust is an indispensable element.

Imagine that a magician tells you that if he stabs you with his knife that nothing is going to happen to you. Will you believe that? Though, you may have seen the magician perform similar magic before, however, you will not let him stab you, even with all the tea in China. This is simply because you do not trust the magician enough to perform that magic on you, and that is because something in your mind tells you that something can go wrong. Thus, you do not want to be a victim of any unforeseen circumstance. That unforeseen circumstance encapsulates your fate. If you allow the magician to perform the magic on you, whatever happens is your fate. Therefore, we believe the things that are beyond our power of understanding and reasoning based on our trust in those things. Without trust faith will be useless. Ask a theist why s/he believes in God or god. The reason goes beyond just faith to include trust in God or god. It is that trust that separates a theist from an atheist with respect to the belief in God or god.

Faith is like a vital organ in our body that keeps us alive. Trust is like a drug that nourishes that vital organ to keep us alive. The moment you run out of that drug, trust, the vital organ, faith, that keeps you alive is damaged, and you are dead. What this means is that you need faith and trust to be alive, and you need them to embrace your fate in life. Have you watched the documentary called Faith and Fate by Berel Wein? The documentary gives a historical account of the Jewish people and their struggles in the twentieth century. It puts into perspective their tragedies, agonies, and victories. Despite the tragedies and agonies that the Jews went through they survived. Your fate is something you have to accept, no matter how it comes. Your faith helps you to defy the trials and tribulations that you are destined to experience in life, and your faith helps you to set a direction to embrace the challenges that life has presented you with. Like, the Jewish people you have to define your purpose in life, you have to understand your destiny, and you have to trust yourself and others. Sometimes your presumption of faith may be the spark of light that sustains you throughout your dark moments in life. It is an integral part of achieving success. Nothing is ever guaranteed in life. Life is full of barriers that block our efforts to achieving the goals that we set for ourselves. This is why we need faith to be able to push ahead and maintain our resilience.

For us to keep our faith alive we must have a defined purpose. Defining your purpose in life is about you understanding the reason why you are here on earth. If you cannot provide a reason for your existence then your life is not worth living. I have met many people who do not know their purpose in life. That is why they do not know what they are doing, that is why they always complain about any situation they find themselves in, that is why they always blame anybody for their misfortunes in life, and that is why they have remained stagnant in life, living off charity. Understanding your destiny is about understanding that some things are meant to happen regardless of how you resist to make them not happen, and some things are not meant to happen even though you wish them to happen. Accepting the challenges that you are faced with is a bold step to dealing with them. You may run away from your personal demons today, but when tomorrow comes they will come knocking, again, on your door. They will not stop knocking until you face them and defeat all of them. But you cannot defeat them if you do not trust in your abilities or you do not have trust in others. Sometimes you cannot do things on your own. We need each other's help. Thus, you cannot work well with other people if you do not trust them. I have seen a lot of people who do not optimize their potentials because they do not trust their abilities.

Imagine when you were a toddler learning how to walk. The first time you took that bold step to stand on your feet and make that move to walk you staggered and fell down. You continued to try to walk until your motion was stabilized and you became mobile. What if as a toddler you did not trust in your ability to try to walk? Perhaps your mobility would have been impaired. This is what happens when you always limit yourself, when you always say you cannot do something because you do not think you can do it, or when you cast doubts on your potentials. When you do not trust yourself, you are definitely not going to trust other people. You have missed many opportunities that would have changed your life because you do not trust anybody. But, how can you possibly live without trusting yourself or anybody?

Faith does not always come with reason. This means that faith is not always rational. Life is unpredictable. Thus, you cannot have all the reasons in the world before you believe in something. Imagine you are a little girl playing with your sister in the snow. Suddenly you fall down. The more you try to get up on your own the more you fall. Your sister will not help you, so you decide not to try anymore, but sit on the snow. Then your father comes out, you are happy that your saviour has arrived, but he insists that you get up yourself and walk towards him. He promises you that you will not fall, but your cheeky sister reminds you of how many times that you have tried and fallen. You ignore your sister and follow your instinct, which tells you to get up and walk because your father says that you will not fall. To your sister's surprise, you walked on the snow towards your father without falling down, and he gave you a big hug. You took that decision to get up and walk not only because you had faith in yourself, but also because you had faith in your father's words, which somehow reawakened your faith in yourself. Your faith was reinforced by your trust in your father. Sometimes people around us can reawaken our faith in ourselves at the periods when our faith seems to have become weak. This is why we must trust ourselves and others. Whatever challenge it is that you are facing in your life just promise yourself that you cannot lose faith in your ability to overcome that challenge. You must always keep your faith alive. But, you have to trust in order to keep your faith alive. With faith and trust you will be able to embrace your fates in life, no matter in what forms they come. Therefore, you should have faith, have trust and embrace your fates. That is the only way to live.

CHAPTER 7

Family vs. Friends

THE TERM FAMILY is a complex concept and its understanding is inherently complicated. When you think about the term family there are many things that come to mind. There are things like family lineage, birth family, birth order, marriage and sibling rivalries. To some people family is about blood ties. Here relationship is bound by blood. Sometimes it seems like a bond that cannot be broken and other times it seems like a covenant that one must eternally be obligated to fulfill. The family ritual has to be maintained. To some people family goes beyond blood ties. Friends become families because blood ties mean nothing and do not matter. Here relationship is about trust and rapport. What matters is the love from the strong connection you build with people. Sometimes you are strongly connected to friends than the people you have blood ties with. Your friendship with them becomes a bond that cannot be broken. Sometimes that friendship becomes a covenant that must remain binding. The key word for you is not family but love, and love means trust and vice versa.

However, whichever way you view family, whether in terms of blood ties or otherwise, I think your view is valid and as such merits respect. What matters the most is love and trust. Without love and trust family or friendship means nothing. Most times our perception of family is shaped by the experiences that we have had in the course of our lives. These experiences come in different forms. They can be betrayals, in which case we suffered several betrayals from the people we share blood ties with. As a result, we have lost our trusts in them. Therefore, people, who earn our trust, are the people that we call friends. Come rain and sunshine they stand by us. Thus, the love and trust become our symbol of family. Also, the experiences can be neglect or abandonment, in which case we were neglected or abandoned at the early stages of our lives by the people that are meant to be families based on blood ties. So, we grew up not having any relationship with them, rather with the people that nature brought into our lives as friends. Thus, those friends become the families that we never had. The experiences can be sheer changes in our orientation about life, in which case we have grown to learn and understand life in a much different and better way.

My perception of family and friendship has changed significantly over the years. I think that family goes beyond blood ties. Family is about love, it is about trust, it is about rapport, it is about building connection, and it is about building lasting relationships. It does not matter to me who I build this love, or rapport, or connection, or relationship with. What matters to me is that I am surrounded by someone or people that I call family, and I call them family because of the love and trust we share, and not because we have the same blood flowing in our veins. However, blood ties do matter to me. It is important to love and build trust, rapport and connection with the people you have blood ties with, but it is equally important to understand that sometimes there are circumstances in life that will make blood ties to be less important to you. Therefore, I am not downplaying the relevance of blood ties or suggesting subversion of friends over the people nature has made you family with; rather I am advocating for love and trust over everything. Family should signify love, trust, rapport, and connection. That is the premise of my perception about family. Therefore, I ask: when blood ties are conflict with genuine love, what takes priority?

Indeed, family means different things to different people. There are people, who think that family is something that is eternal, in which case the blood ties are meant to flow forever, regardless of what happens. I am often tempted to wonder if this locus is not deliberately twisted to evoke an existence of a bond or covenant that should be eternally binding, regardless of whether the relationships that come out of it are pivoted to benefit some people while the other people suffer. I am tempted to think that family has become a doctrine that people invoke whenever it suits them to satisfy their desires. This comes with some sort of order that is often placed on us to make us subservient to people's

CHUKWUMA JULIUS OKONKWO

whims and caprices. You are often compelled to obey whatever your family says and accept however things turn out.

Imagine you were abandoned by your parents when you were born. Luckily, someone picked you up from the bin where your parents had dumped you and sent you to an orphanage. Subsequently, you were adopted by a couple, who nurtured and raised you into an adult. Now you have become somebody, out of nobody. Suddenly, your biological mother discovered you. She told you stories about how she made the decision to leave you at the bin, she told you that she could not let you die of hunger, so that decision was the best option to keep you alive because she knew someone would pick you up and look after you, she told you how your biological father impregnated her and abandoned her, she told you all her gory experience of carrying the pregnancy and giving birth to you at a nearby garage, and she told you how she had been looking for you ever since her conditions changed and became better. But, she wanted you back as her child. She evoked those memories to make you believe that she is your mother, and also to have you back as her child. She does not care that you have parents now and most importantly a family. All she cares about is the blood ties that say that she is your mother and you are her child. While some would argue that the couples who nurtured and raised you into the person you have become now are your family, not what the biological test says, others would argue that blood ties trump everything and nothing can change that, except death; hence you should leave the parents you have known all your life and go back to your biological mother. So, I ask: when biology conflicts with genuine love, what takes priority?

The above story illustrates the situations many people are into. It can come in different forms. It may be that people who have never been there for you suddenly appear in your life, perhaps when things are working out well for you. Then they evoke memories of the past to tell you about the blood ties. They remember you share the same surname with them and remind you of family traditions. But, biology does not always mean family. It may be a process that leads to an emergence of life, but it does not necessarily mean an emergence of family. Family is about making sacrifices. If your biological parents or siblings or relatives cannot make sacrifices when the needs arise then the word family has lost its essence and relevance. They do not deserve to be called family. If you cannot make sacrifices to your parents or siblings or relatives, you too do not deserve to be called family. I am often tempted to think that family has become a notion implanted in our minds to compel us to conform to some beliefs, perhaps the beliefs that even when your family causes you pains you should tighten up your teeth and endure the pains because family is something inseparable. Under this notion we are forced to believe that we can make something that is imperfect perfect. But, family is full of contradictions and imperfections. These contradictions and imperfections are sometimes irreparable and irredeemable, and as such the reasons why family is separable.

Family is a more complex concept than friendship. People often say that you can choose your friends but you cannot choose your family because your family is divinely chosen for you. That notion makes it somehow easy to get rid of friends that you do not want in your life but difficult to get rid of relatives, even when they consistently cause you pains. In other words, once you are born you are stuck with your family forever. I am tempted to think that, that is another notion that people often evoke to make family look like an innate oath that must not be broken, regardless of what happens in life. What happens when your family does not understand and accept you for who you are, but you have friends who understand and accept you for who you are?

Imagine you are gay and your family abhors gay people. You decide one day to come out because you cannot hide it anymore. Then your family disavows you. You become a pariah and all the love they have for you is taken back because of your sexual orientation. The persecution becomes unbearable, and then you relocate to somewhere else where you can start a new life. There, in your new location, you are blessed with a friend who accepts and loves you for who you are. Over the years you have built strong rapport and relationship with your friend. The relationship has grown to become bonds you both share, and the bonds have become unbreakable. For you, your friend is the only family you have, even though there are no blood ties. Your friend has been there for you throughout your trials and tribulations and you have been there for your friend as well. Suddenly, there is an earthquake in a certain region. But, because you work with a humanitarian organization you are dispatched to a rescue mission in that region. Then you are faced with two patients, one is a little girl and the other is a male in his late forties. Both patients have severely lost blood and as such they need urgent transfusion. There is no blood bank in place yet, it will take time to set up the blood bank and get people to donate blood. If there is no transfusion in few minutes both patients will die. Their hope of survival is only if some people within your team can donate their blood. But, there is a problem. Their blood group is O negative, meaning that they cannot receive from any blood group, except O negative. There is only one person in your team who can save them. That person is you. You are happy to donate your blood, but you can donate to only one person, otherwise you will become blood deficient and cannot work. That is the risk your organization cannot take.

However, there is something about both patients, apart from the blood group compatibility, that struck your mind to check their identities. To your surprise the male patient is your biological brother and the little girl is your friend's niece. That is your friend who has become your family. The little girl is the only child of her parents and you remember how your friend had talked about her. Saving her life will mean more than the world to your friend. By extension it will mean saving a family. But, you have your biological brother's life hanging in the balance. Now you have to make a decision about who to save. What will inform your decision? Is it the blood ties that you have with your brother who for decades has not been your family, or is it the friendship that you have built with your friend who has become your family? The decision is yours to make. If you choose to save the life of the little girl based on the friendship, rapport, love and trust you have built with your friend, your decision merits respect. If you choose to throw all that away and save your biological brother's life based on blood ties your decision merits respect too. For me, family is not blood, but love, trust, rapport, connection, and sacrifice.

CHAPTER 8

Giving vs Exploitation

IN THE ACT of giving there are three categories of people. There are givers, takers, and matchers. There are few givers in the world, today. Majority of the people you meet are takers and matchers. Who are the givers, takers, and matchers? Givers are those who give without expecting anything in return. They love to give because it is in their DNA (Deoxyribonucleic acid) to give. They enjoy giving because they want to make positive impacts on people. They are inspired to give because by giving they never lack. Givers do not give for any particular reason other than their desire to make a difference. They are addicted to giving and as such giving has become their way of life. You cannot stop them from giving because they are always driven by the spirit of giving. Takers are those who always want to receive. When they give, eventually, they want to receive more than they have given. They are addicted to receiving and as such they see every opportunity as a chance to exploit others. They live with a poorly shaped mindset that nothing goes for nothing, so they do not give without expecting something in return. They do not contribute to anything that does not benefit them. They are always driven by the spirit of taking. Matchers are hybrid of givers and takers. They give and they take. They are always strategic and calculative about what and how they give. They always balance what they give and what they receive. They see giving as a means to expand their lots. The borderline between them and takers is that they can be driven by the spirit of giving.

By now you must have known the category that defines you. Giving is a virtue that not everyone possesses. Giving is an act of help or assistance. When you give you are helping to change something or somebody's life, or you are contributing towards a greater purpose.

Giving is a way of making difference. But, we have attached strings to the concept of giving. This is the reason why people do not help without expecting something in return. Thus, an act of giving has become an act of exploitation and as such a business opportunity to be exploited. These days people give terms and conditions before they agree to help you with anything. The act of giving has lost its natural meaning, which is to give and expect nothing in return.

I grew up from a background where there are many matchers. Imagine a poor kid who is driven by the passion to acquire university education. But, this poor kid cannot be sponsored to the university by those who have the resources to do that because they have calculated that the course that the kid wants to study has no relevance to their line of business. So giving the poor kid access to university education is about calculating how the kid will contribute in return to your investment on the kid's university education. This contribution will involve the kid working for your company where you can exploit his or her knowledge and skills to expand your business. Imagine an industrious young man who is not interested in going to the university because he has a natural talent for business. He does not have the capital to start his own business, but he has relatives who have the capital that he needs to start his business. Unfortunately, the young man cannot get help from his family for the little capital that he needs to start his business because his decision not to go to university is perceived as an aberration to the family ritual – a ritual that everyone must go to university and become a graduate. So giving is about maintaining the family ritual. Imagine that life is kicking you hard in the butt with many challenges that you cannot count. You have a friend that can help alleviate your situation. But, your friend will not out-rightly help you without some form of assurance that you are going to return the favour whenever it is needed from you. So helping people has become assets that we acquire in the form of favours that people owe us whenever we help them with something.

The world is in a mess partly because there are too many takers and matchers and few givers. When you think about hunger and poverty in the world today, it certainly blows your mind. We have too many people below the poverty line and we have few people living in affluence. I worked for a guy who believes that the only way to end hunger and poverty in the world is by the rich people using their wealth to lift up the poor people. Many people share this view, but the problem is in lifting people up without any strings attached. I think the reason people attach strings when they are helping other people is because they do not see the act of giving as a responsibility. The world is framed in a way that everything is about business and nobody is responsible for anybody. The rich people believe that they are not responsible for the poor people. So whenever a rich person is helping a poor person it is often about a business opportunity that must be exploited. This is why you see that when people are helping other people they always think they are doing them a favour, which must be returned someday, if not immediately.

Imagine what will happen if all the rich people in the world decide that it is their responsibility to lift up the poor people within their society or community. You will see that there will be no strings attached because there will be more sincerity of purpose, you will see genuine act of giving because people will see act of giving as what it truly is, rather than as an act of exploiting business opportunity, you will see significant changes in the lives of people around the world, you will see people moving to the next levels of their lives, you will see increase in the number of people giving to change humanity, and you will see the world become a better and freer place to live in.

It is often said that givers never lack. How truthful is that? If that is true why do we have more takers and matchers than givers? Indeed, givers do not lack because when you give genuinely you endear people to you. People admire and respect givers. Because people admire and respect you they will always support you. By that you will build strong relationships with people. People will only seek to mow you down if you give and exploit them, and in that case you are not a giver in real sense. We live in a world where people speak more with less action. People only want to stand and talk, but they are not willing to walk. This is why many people know and believe that givers do not lack, but they prefer to be recipients. Imagine you are a rich and influential person in your society or community and you are helping to lift up many people in different ways you can. You are using your wealth, expertise, experiences and networks. There is no exploitation and there are no return favours. It is just an act of giving to humanity. By giving you are expanding the givers circle and making the top less lonely for yourself. The more people you lift up the more people there will be at the top and the less lonely you will be at the top. This means that you are not giving to remain the sole giver, but you are giving to create other givers who will join you in giving to others. When you lift somebody up and that person lifts someone else up and that continues in that sequence you have created a circle of givers within your society or community. Then your act of giving has transformed the entire society or community. That is the big picture you have created. However, most times we see the big picture, but we prefer to follow the path that will only satisfy our self-interests.

There is a story in the Bible (Luke 12:13 – 21) called the parable of the rich fool. It is about a rich man who was blessed with all the wealth he desired. He was so rich that he did not know what to do with his wealth. All he could think of was how to become extravagant, he thought he could demolish his storehouse and build new bigger storehouses that would accommodate more wealth, and he thought he could just sit and enjoy his wealth all by himself. Suddenly, God, his creator, disgusted by his greed and selfishness, decided to take his life. He could not live to enjoy his riches as he had planned. This parable is a reflection of the greed and selfishness that characterize relationships among people these days, particularly the relationship between the rich and the poor. It is also a reflection of the reasons why most people have become takers and matchers, instead of givers. The world is predominantly takers and matchers because of sheer greed of people. Because of greed, when natural disasters, like hurricane or flood or earthquake, happen you see individuals and organizations exploiting the bad conditions of the victims to their private interests, hiding under the cover of rescue mission. It is because of greed that many developed countries, hiding under the cover of development aid or assistance, impoverish many developing countries. Greed is the reason why multinational companies damage natural environments in many developing countries and hide under the cover of corporate social responsibility to commit more damages. It is because of sheer greed that many rich and successful people, including politicians, business leaders, academics, celebrities in the entertainment world, and religious leaders, hiding under the cover of giving back to the society, exploit the vast majority of people in societies and communities to their personal interests. Until we disrobe ourselves of this garment of greed and selfishness that we wear every day, act of giving will always mean a business opportunity that must be exploited.

CHUKWUMA JULIUS OKONKWO

CHAPTER 9

Intolerance vs. Tolerance

IN 2013, I wrote a poem titled 'Intolerance'. That was inspired by my late father's memoir, which he wrote in 1973. Before I wrote the poem, I had read that memoir uncountable times right from when I was a kid, but reading it again in 2013 inspired me in a different way words could not express. The things that I saw and read on social media pushed me to write the poem. I was worried about how incidents of terrorism were twisted on social media.

Indeed, social media can be a blessing and a curse. It depends on how it is exploited. Since the invention of social media, possibly in 1997, individuals, companies, multinationals and even countries have exploited the benefits provided by social media. These benefits are numerous and in-exhaustive. However, social media platforms have been exploited in many negative ways that cannot be emphasized enough in this chapter. Social media platforms, for example, Facebook and Twitter have become outlets for display of intolerance, as opposed to building cordial relationships, and even acquiring knowledge.

In 2013, there were many terrorist attacks across the world. In fact, several global reports revealed that terrorism heightened astronomically, in terms of number of deaths and attacks, in that year. All those attacks were perpetrated differently by Islamic militant groups, such as ISIS (Islamic State of Iraq and Syria), al-Qaeda, Boko Haram and the Taliban. From Karachi in Pakistan, to Taji in Iraq, to Damascus in Syria, to Mogadishu in Somalia, to Kano in Nigeria, to Kidal in Mali, to Boston in the United States, and to Woolwich in the United Kingdom, there were terrorist attacks and deaths of innocent people. Across social media, I saw how divided human beings had become, I could not help, but let my ink flow and lay bare my emotions and worries.

Today, Islamic religion is under attack as a violent religion; Muslims are continuously labeled terrorists; Christianity is under severe persecution; atheists now think that making a caricature of other people's religion and their revered religious prophets is pleasant; and people have become defensive in an attempt to preserve their religious faith.

Intolerance is surely a disease; the worst disease I have ever seen in my life. It continues to damage souls. People do not know how to cure themselves of this disease; they do not even care about the cure. Sadly, intolerance seems to have become a way of life, and people feel comfortable walking around in the garment of intolerance. There are religious wars and crisis across the world. Islamic religion is often attacked as a violent religion. Muslims are often labeled terrorists and have continued to face stereotypes. Christianity is also under attack. Christians are often persecuted and deprived of their religious rights. There are many caricatures of religious prophets, like Jesus Christ and Prophet Mohammed. A Christian thinks it is okay to speak ill about other religions and prophets because s/he does not agree with their teachings. A Muslim speaks ill about other religions and prophets because s/he does not share the same beliefs. A Muslim is glorified for murdering a fellow human being in the name of religion. These are all acts of intolerance. They show how deep intolerance as a disease has damaged many minds. They show how deep the gangrene caused by intolerance has eaten the fabrics of religions.

Intolerance has created religious borderlines within the same religion. Pentecostals, Roman Catholics and Anglicans launch low blows on each other because they see themselves as different denominations and have different understandings of the same religion. Shiites and Sunnis Muslims attack each other because they see themselves as different groups with different ideals of the same religion. Whenever there is a terrorist attack, the verbal and written attacks on social media and the narratives on mainstream media show how carnivorous human minds have become. The so-called religious people adore revenge so much that revenge now tastes like honey in their mouths. Defending religion has become the ultimate goal of worshippers rather than living it. There is no tolerance because intolerance has put fetters on tolerance.

CHUKWUMA JULIUS OKONKWO

Intolerance fuels religious crisis across the world and inspires all kinds of discrimination – racial or sexual. People judge what they do not understand and hate what they do not agree with. The chords of intolerance have entangled many souls; hence the foundation of many religions shakes. In the presence of the so-called religious leaders the surge of destruction to the fabrics of religion multiplies. They do not teach how to live a religion, but how to defend it. This is why people have ascribed to themselves the role of God; to judge and to condemn. As a result, people are no longer satisfied with their own battles as human beings; rather they fight God's battles. This is why we see human beings being beheaded in the name of blasphemy, we see children being offensively abused and even killed in the name of evil spirit, we see human beings being blatantly dehumanized in the name of deliverance, we see people ostracize their families and friends in the name of adhering to religious principles, and we see people being treated as outcasts because of their sexual orientation.

Intolerance constantly destroys the essence of who we are as human beings. Intolerance erodes the values that make us human beings. With our own hands we have used intolerance to break the umbilical cord that unites us to a common humanity. On the altar of intolerance we have murdered the spirit of ubuntu. We now seek intolerance like intoxicants because we cannot stand each other anymore. We have become so complacent with intolerance that it has become an irresistible honeypot. We do not see any wrong with it anymore. But, no religion teaches us to be intolerant; rather religion teaches us how to be tolerant. No religion empowers anyone to fight God's battle. God fights his own battles. No Holy Book gives anyone the legitimacy to play the role of God; to judge and to condemn. The court of justice has the legitimacy to decide how someone who has blasphemed should be punished. It is certainly not your call. Children who are labeled evil-children and as such are abused, killed, or banished do not deserve such treatments. They have the right to live. No religion gives anyone the right to speak ill of another person's religion. Religion is not a passport to heaven or wherever you wish to go to in after life. No religion gives anyone the right to speak ill about God or his revered prophets or servants. Even you the atheists, who make caricature of religions and revered prophets, you do not have the right to do so, no matter how liberally-oriented you claim the world should become. These are what intolerance has forced people to do and become. Intolerance has forced human beings to play the role God and that of the court of justice. Intolerance has made us to hate each other. Intolerance has turned us against ourselves. But, we must purge ourselves the poisons that intolerance has implanted in us.

Intolerance is a real problem in the world and we must see it that way. All the crises that we see in the world today revolve around intolerance. This is why we must cure ourselves of intolerance that we suffer as sickness. I am worried about how fast intolerance has taken reign over tolerance, I am worried about how intolerance has eaten deep into the fabrics of our souls, I am really worried about the future of the world in the hands of intolerance. That I am a Christian does not give me the right to speak ill about a religion or prophet I do not believe in. That you are a Muslim does not give you the right to speak ill about a religion or prophet you do not believe in. That somebody speaks ill about a religion we worship or a prophet we believe so much in does not give us the right to play the role of God. That we have different views about someone's sexual orientation should not make us to judge and condemn. We are temporarily here to obey God's command by doing his will. Intolerance is certainly not his will. The Holy Books that we derive our faith from do not command us to judge or condemn or kill. They preach love and peace. If we truly believe in the words that we read from the Holy Books, then we must live and let others live. We must live religion. Living religion is about loving each other. Loving each other is about being tolerant of one another and accommodating each other. We are all flawed in the presence of our creator.

Intolerance is not an act of nature, rather it is something that we created by ourselves. As a disease that we are infected with, we have to cure our intolerance. The cure is in our hands. But, we have to care about intolerance for us to be able to cure it. We have to discuss our intolerance with each other to be able to deal with it. The cure is the opposite – tolerance. Being tolerant of other people's beliefs, religion, opinions, orientation, and culture is certainly the pathway to purging ourselves of the poisons that intolerance has implanted in us and the world of its numerous crises. We should open up our hearts and let tolerance triumph over our intolerance. Tolerance is about acceptance and accommodation. It is fundamental to our existence as human beings and the way we should approach life. Tolerance is when a Christian looks a Muslim in the face and sees no religion but a human being s/he is comfortable to live with, and vice versa. Tolerance is when a Jew sees in the face of a Buddhist no indifference but a persuasion to save humanity. Tolerance is when a Shiite looks a Sunnis in the eyes and sees no distinctiveness. Tolerance is when a Catholic looks a Protestant in the face and sees no denomination. Tolerance is when human beings are joined together by a simple and common purpose; to live and let others live. Salvation is not about attachment to religious beliefs, or multiplicity of religion, rather it is about tolerance and singleness of purpose of why we are human beings. That purpose is to love and live. To love we must tolerate others. To live we must let others live. Tolerance means saying no to intolerance. It is purging ourselves of what intolerance has made us. Tolerance knows no religion or race or creed or colour or sexual orientation. Tolerance is just being humane and living like a human being.

CHAPTER 10

Life is a Ring: We Fall and We Rise

INDEED, LIFE IS full of challenges. Show me the guy who has never experienced any challenge in life and I will prove to you that the guy does not exist on this planet, earth. Nobody is immune from life's challenges. There is no best way to describe life and the challenges that it brings. For me, life is a situational phenomenon. This means that life is approached differently based on your situations, which are different from others. Thus, life deals different situations to different people. Truly, people face different challenges in different situations and even within the same situations, sometimes. Take pregnancy, for example, it is the same phenomenon for women. But, the challenges that come with pregnancy may or may not be the same for all women. This is why there are different approaches to life and its challenges. It is different strokes for different folks.

When I was a young kid, I used to watch a lot of wrestling championships. Each wrestling match that I watched I never thought about it beyond the ring. I watched wrestling because it was entertaining, even though people usually got injured during the wrestling match. I was always carried away by the fantasy of the game that I never believed the injuries were real. Now that I have grown into an adult, I still watch wrestling, but not with the same enthusiasm, like when I was a young kid. I think about wrestling beyond the rings now. Like wresting, watching boxing was the same feelings when I was growing up and the same feelings now that I have grown up.

I see life through the lens of the wrestling and boxing rings. When you watch wrestling or boxing you see punch from opponents, flying

CHUKWUMA JULIUS OKONKWO

like bullets. Think for a second about life as a wrestling or boxing ring. Here your opponent is life. Did you see the punch coming? There is no certainty that you will see the punch coming, sometimes you do because you anticipate them and dodge them, and sometimes you do not, because they just come unexpectedly. I see life's challenges as the punches that life throws at us. If you anticipate the punches, you will make plans to dodge or navigate them, but sometimes they just come unexpectedly. But, regardless of whether you anticipated them or not you will still have to deal with them. Every punch comes with strings of pain. When life throws its heavy punches, the blow hits us, it seems like the gate of pain is opened, the pains run through our muscles quickly, like the smokes from a deadly missile that hits its target, and then the pains go straight to our heart. There in our heart the pains hurt much, then to our head, and we begin to think that our world has crumbled. But, life must continue and you must face your problems.

When you watch a wrestling match, you see wrestlers throw punches at their opponents; you see wrestlers kick their opponents very hard; you see wrestlers squeeze their opponents' head so tight as if they want to strangle them to death; and wrestlers do those things with no atom of mercy. It is the same story with a boxing match. Boxers do not show mercy to their opponents. They punch the opponent where it hurts the most. This is because either a wrestler or boxer is certainly in the ring to win. Also, like any other game, in a wrestling or boxing match there is something at stake; it could be the huge amount of money or just the fame that comes with winning the game. In a wrestling or boxing match it is not always the guy who throws the most punch or they guy who kicks the hardest kick or the guy who attacks in the most violent way that wins. Sometimes it is the guy who received the most beating, kicking and squeezing that ends up winning the wrestling or boxing match. The victory comes when the guy who has been beaten to the ground makes a comeback. The guy on the ground makes a comeback because he is able to endure the pains from the punches, the kicks and the squeezes, perhaps the fear of losing or the sense of winning what is at stake motivates him to rise. When this happens it is always a bitter pill for the other guy to swallow.

I have seen a lot of wrestlers who came from the ground their opponent had beaten them to win the wrestling match. Examples of such cases abound; it is not uncommon in wrestling championships. When I think beyond the wrestling rings I see the story behind the punch, the kick, and the squeeze. When I link the wrestling rings to life and its challenges I see the connection. The wrestling game is just the reality of life, and that is that we are punched, then we fall, we endure the pains from the punch, and we rise. The punch, the kick, and the squeeze bring the best out of wrestlers. They remember what is at stake too, and could be inspired by the fear of losing or the sense of winning. Picture your life as a ring and the challenges that life deals you as your opponent for a second, again. No matter how hard it seems to rise, always remember what is at stake. Sometimes there is an illusion that everything is gone, so there is nothing at stake. There is always something at stake, it can be anything, and that should motivate you to rise and face your challenges. Personally, I have been beaten to the ground several times by challenges in life. In some of those times I felt barren and hopeless. But, I was nudged by the presumption of faith that everything would be fine. I am always inspired by what is at stake. It is easier to give up than face the challenges. Giving up may be an easy option, certainly, it is not inspiring.

Now imagine you are a little girl and your parents have a pony. You love to climb up and down the pony. Your daddy always puts you on the pony. One day your parents are not at home and you want to play your usual game of climbing up and down the pony. The pony is tied to a tree. Your elder brother does not want to help you climb up the pony. You try several times to climb the pony, but you fail. The more you try, the more you fail to climb the pony. You keep trying. Sometimes it seems that you are nearly up on the pony, but when you try to turn your right foot around to sit on the pony you suddenly lose balance and then you are back to square one. You have tried so hard several times to climb up the pony that your body is beginning to hurt, yet you are unsuccessful. When you look the pony in the eyes you wish it could just bend for you to climb up, but the pony does not understand your agony. Then you pushed yourself one more time, this time fate is on your side, and there you are sitting on the pony brimming with smiles. Despite the pains on your body when you were trying to climb up the pony you persevered. Now you are extremely happy that you finally did it. But, if you had given up when it seemed like you would never climb up the pony, you would not have been sitting on the pony with joy in your heart and smiles all over your face, perhaps you would have been somewhere feeling sorry for yourself and regretting why you even tried in the first place. Hard work and perseverance got you up there. This is the reality of life. Giving up may cost you the joy and happiness that are waiting for you at the end of your struggles. That one more push might be the life changer for you.

Our challenges in life are numerous and as such may differ. The punch, the kick, and the squeeze, all come in different forms and sizes, but the objectives are the same – to knock us down, to make us powerless, to make us vulnerable, and above all to defeat us. Sometimes we may resort to self-comfort by thinking that life is unfair to only us. Certainly, that is not the case because life challenges are loads that everybody carries on their shoulders. As life punches you in the face with unemployment, it punches your neighbour in the chest with a life threatening sickness. As life kicks you in the butt with no income to pay your bills, it steps on your colleague's stomach with infertility. As life squeezes your neck with constant failures in your examinations, it squeezes your friend's arms with unsuccessful job interviews. As life deals you a double blow with deaths of loved ones and setbacks in business, it belts a triple problem to another person. Rather than thinking that you are alone with your life challenges, think more about the things that are at stake. Do not fall into the illusion trap that everything is gone. There is always something left. Under the debris of your destroyed home you may still find your gold.

The daily challenges that we face are the punch, the kick and the squeeze that life gives us. These challenges pose as barriers to our goals and visions in life. We must not let them defeat us. Let us be driven by presumption of faith that everything will eventually be fine. When you watch a wrestling or boxing match and see wrestlers or boxers who have been beaten to the ground make a comeback, let it inspire you, do not be afraid to walk in their shoes. The punches that life hits our faces with should bring out the best in us, the pains that we experience when life kicks us in the butt should bring more determination out of us, and the pangs of pains when life squeezes some vital parts in our body should make us stronger than we were before. Do not lose sight of what is at stake. Let it be your motivation and inspiration.

Life challenges can come like a hurricane. The headwinds of losses, disappointments, failures, regrets, and setbacks come like volcanic eruptions shattering what we have planned to achieve or acquired, or aspire to become. Then there comes the flood of pains flowing throwing our veins and flooding our eyes with tears that we somehow cannot dry enough, no matter how hard we try. But, you must look beyond how broken your challenges in life have left you. You should always make a comeback no matter how hard life has beaten you to the ground. You cannot afford to fall and not rise again.

CHAPTER 11

New Year Resolution

O N NEW YEAR'S Eve there is often a ritual that people perform – a ritual of personal reflection on how the year has gone. During this reflection people take stock of their actions in the ending year and pledge to improve in the incoming year. There is no single way to define New Year resolution. But, there is clarity on what it involves. It involves decision-making, making plans, or sacrificing something.

There is a wrong notion that a lot of people have about New Year resolution, and that is that things change or improve automatically. Most times people rehearse their New Year resolutions as if such a rehearsal will translate into results immediately. Most people do not realize that mere New Year resolutions do not change or improve anything, but actions reflected in hard work change or improve things. You can sit and rehearse your New Year resolutions as many times as you want, but if you do not put in hard work to execute those decisions or plans, or make those sacrifices, you are definitely not going to achieve any positive result regardless of how exciting they may seem. The key thing is not the litany of your resolutions, but your ability to execute actions towards achieving your resolutions. Often times we are so caught up in the frenzy of making New Year resolutions that we forget that what really matters is the effort committed towards executing those plans or decisions. Thus, power of execution is the real thing and game changer. This is why you should be driven by hard work and task execution and not by the list of your New Year resolutions.

Any New Year resolution without any hard work put into action is nothing but an illusion. It is just like waiting for manna to fall from heaven. I used to have a friend, who was a chain smoker. Every New

Year's Eve he would resolve to quit his smoking habit. But, he would smoke a lot on the night of the eve and then believe that he would wake up in the morning of the New Year a full brand new person with no urge to smoke ever again. This is just like a child who plants a flower in the garden and believes that when morning comes the flower will produce blooms. My friend did not understand that New Year's Eve is just like any other night, except that it leads to another year. Most people do not understand this too. The New Year's Day is just an annex of the New Year's Eve. It is only by a stretch of the imagination that you would expect my friend, who had been on a smoking spree on the New Year's Eve and as such had inundated his system with nicotine, to quit his smoking habit on the stroke of a New Year resolution. Until my friend realized that an action encapsulated into hard work was what he needed to quit smoking, he was always making failed New Year resolutions. The logic here is that simply making a list of New Year resolutions does not actually mean that you are going to achieve your desired positive outcomes. What guarantees positive outcomes is the level of hard work that you put into executing your plans or decisions.

I believe in making New Year resolution, but I believe strongly that it should be backed by executing actions; otherwise it is a fruitless exercise. I remember being asked few years ago by a friend what my New Year resolution for that year was, and I replied that it was just to make mistakes. I remember how surprised she looked when I said that. Obviously, she had expected something more conventional. But, I am not conventional. Though my New Year resolution has always been to make mistakes, but every year I do add something unconventional to it. I have been making mistakes. I have been learning from my mistakes. I will never stop making mistakes. I will never stop learning from my mistakes. This is a lesson that growing into an adult taught me. And it has become my personal litany.

Growing into an adult often comes with mixed feelings. It may be the feeling of happiness that comes with becoming an adult. This happiness comes with a sense of maturity and independence. This sense of maturity takes you to a world of consciousness where you begin to be mindful of the things that happen around you. In this world of

CHUKWUMA JULIUS OKONKWO

consciousness you begin to seek clarity on virtually everything. Then the things that ultimately matter to you begin to unfold as your hunger for clarity increases. Also, growing into an adult may be the fear that comes with becoming an adult. In clinical psychology it has been investigated and proved that the fear of adulthood makes some people not to want to become adults. Indeed, this fear can be wide ranging. Adult life comes with a sense of independence. The annual ritual of personal reflection upon which New Year resolution is premised is part of this independence in adult life. This does not suggest in any way that children do not make New Year resolutions, certainly they do, rather it implies that the ritual is predominantly an adult thing.

For me, growing into an adult comes with the fear of making mistakes and making a resolution to overcome my fears by making more mistakes. I grew up being averse to mistakes. That was because I was afraid of failing. My fear of failing enclosed me in my own shell, which obviously was comfortable for me at that time. At home, in school, in church, at social events, and in fact everywhere, I lived in my own shell, where I was always afraid of trying new things because I thought that doing something new would always come with mistakes and then failure. My fear of making mistakes and failing made me less adventurous. Inside that shell it appeared that my parents were making all the decisions for me; I never felt ready to hold the bag.

Indeed, making mistakes comes with costs, fears and regrets. However, mistakes do not kill. This is another lesson growing into adult taught me. I wish I had learnt that as a kid. Mistakes mold you into better clay of your kind. Making mistakes is rewarding. This is because there is a lesson inherent in every mistake. Every mistake provides big opportunity to perform better than the previous attempt. William Shakespeare in his famous work, 'As You Like It', described the world as a stage where we play different roles. At some point some people discover themselves while others are already established. At another point some people want to do something absolutely new. As human beings we cannot run away from making mistakes. Uncertainty is man's greatest agony. We wish we knew what would happen tomorrow and certain about next second. If we were certain about life or knew everything, surely we would not make mistakes; hence everything would be perfect. But, there is no perfection and certainty in life. The only thing that is certain is death and the only place that perfection exists is in the mind.

I live in the world of mistakes, where I embrace every mistake with a naked heart and open arms. In this world I have been trying new things, I have been making mistakes, I have been failing, and most importantly, I have been learning and changing myself and my world. In today's world, virtually everybody aspire to make a change. The drive to change the world has heightened like we have never seen before. However, a lot of people are afraid of making mistakes. The costs, fears and regrets that come from making mistakes hold people back from trying new things and executing the ideas in their heads. As a result people are held back from conquering their world. I have come across many young people, who are full of ideas. But, at the end of the day the ideas expire in their heads because they fail to execute them. Most times I am tempted to argue that ideas do not matter as much as they are preached. For me, what matters the most is the power of execution. This is not to discountenance ideas in toto; rather it is to suggest that ideas without execution are useless. Everybody has ideas, but what separates people is the power of execution. I believe firmly that if you want to make a change, you will be prepared to make mistakes. In the arc of daily life struggles making mistakes can lead to fortunes when taken in (your) stride. Whatever it is you are doing while you are still on this stage called life, do not be afraid to make mistakes and execute ideas.

In 2014, I met a guy in Dubai, who told me that his goal in life was just to live and enjoy life. That inspired me. I added to my annual resolution to always live on the positive side of life and enjoy life to the fullest. That mind-set has always helped me to waddle through my stormy years in life. No doubts, life is not devoid of regrets. In fact, life has never worked out for me, like a birthday party, the way I planned it. I have failed more than I have achieved success. All my life it has been struggles. Indeed, if you were to write a script about my life the plot would be struggles. But, I always stand on my feet and dance. My struggles in life have shown me the ugliest side of life, life has knocked me down numerous times and has shown me much pains that pains do not taste like pains anymore. Despite all the setbacks I have experienced in life I still survive. No matter how down to the rock bottom life has kicked me to I still find hope within me to bust a gut. With all my regrets I keep smiling. With all my mistakes I keep learning. With all my numerous failures I keep working hard. I persist by presumption of faith that no matter what I am going through in life, no matter the disappointments, and no matter the number of 'no' responses that I get, life will be better with time. Sometimes it does not even get better, but worse, yet my faith carries me through. The same thing should apply to you. You are still growing and learning. You have come a long way, so giving up is not an option, always remember that. Let your faith guide you because faith is an integral part of success in life. Embrace uncertainty because you cannot run away from uncertainty. Let the uncertainty of life inspire you as you look for a change in your life or situation.

CHAPTER 12

The Pangs of Suicide

I MAGINE YOU HAVE a 21 year old son, who is incredibly brilliant. He studies at the university a course only a few people within his age bracket would want to study; he wants to become an astrophysicist. He has multiple scholarships from multinational organizations that cater for his educational needs, so he does not have problems with funding. He is on top of his game when it comes to studying astrophysics. Your son's brilliance tells you that he is going to become the best astrophysicist the world has ever seen. He is not only good at his field of study, but he is also good at other areas, like poetry and football. His style of poetry reminds you of the greatest poets that you have read their works, and nothing in your mind gives you a doubt that your son will become a renowned poet, just like one of his uncles, who was a renowned poet. You have watched him play football. You see how good he is at dribbling and how precise his ball control is. Then you wonder if it will be a great idea to withdraw him from the university and send him to a football academy, because his football skills are extraordinary. You are amazed by your son's multiple talents and you are very proud of his charisma.

One day your son exhibits an episode of mental disorder. You have no idea where the mental illness comes from, because you have no memory of any mental disorder in your family lineage. In your society people do not usually admit that they have mental issues because there is a societal stigma that comes with being mentally ill. This stigma starts from the nuclear family, to the extended family, and to the public. You do not think that your son's episode is a serious one; perhaps your fear of societal stigma dilutes your logical reasoning, so you shrugged off medical diagnosis into your son's episode of mental disorder. You do not talk about it because people do not talk about that. You are comfortable with discussing sex and relationships with your son, but you have never talked about that episode. Thus, within a short period the memory of that episode goes away, it seems like it never happened. Then few years later, that one episode turned into recurring episodes.

Now your son's mental disorder has become worse, he is admitted into a psychiatric hospital. The psychiatrist says the illness has to be managed consistently because it will keep coming back. The treatment starts and your brilliant son receives the treatment. In a short while he is fine and ready to continue with his usual life. But, everybody now knows that he has a mental disorder that needs to be managed. You try your best as a parent by doing the best you can to love and care for him. But, you cannot control the way other people in society treat him. Most times when people say things to him, they do not see the stigma in their words, those things hurt him, but nobody knows how deeply the pangs penetrate his inner soul. He sees himself as a liability to the family because of his mental disorder. Sometimes the treatments he gets from other people, including his other siblings, persuade his conviction that he is actually a liability. That is something he does not want to be. The thought of becoming a pariah in the society that he has lofty ambitions to contribute to changing lives breaks his heart. He cannot stand the mental torture.

On that fateful day, while he was away in school, the incident happened. You receive the news that your son has passed away in a tragic way. He died by his own rope. Your brilliant son has taken his own life. All his multiple talents, extraordinary charisma and beautiful aspirations are gone. Few hours later the news is all over social media. You read the comments and you see how 99% of them are judgmental. You keep asking yourself why he committed suicide, you thought everything was working out well for him, he had multiple scholarships towards his educational needs, he was on top of his class with a cumulative high distinction grade, and he had only one year left to graduate from the university. But, the answers you seek are elusive, there is no lead to the answers, and nothing makes sense to you as to why he committed suicide, except his mental disorder.

Though research tells us that broad range of demographic, social, economic and clinical factors are responsible for why people commit suicide; however, no one can absolutely understand what people who have committed or tried to commit suicide went through when they decided to take their lives, except them. You can only imagine the pains that someone goes through that makes the person want to take his or her life, but you cannot understand those pains. Most times when people commit suicide we call them cowards who are afraid to face their challenges in life, we say they are selfish because they only care about taking their lives and not taking into account how devastated their loved ones would be, and we judge, blame and condemn them. We say all those things because it is convenient for us to say them. We consider only the pains they have left us with and ignore the pains they might have carried on their shoulders for long; the pains that we, perhaps, contributed to. I have lost a brother to suicide. When I received the news that he had taken his own life, it was difficult for me to come to terms with the reality that he actually did it. Then I was abroad studying. I knew that looking for answers as to why he committed suicide would be a wild goose chase, so I consoled myself with the belief that someday, which I do not know when that day will be, everything would make sense. In the last poem that he wrote before he committed suicide he said that he knew he was destined to take that path. For him suicide was his fate and he accepted his fate with all his brave heart. And he died by his own rope and on his own terms.

One of the things that I have learnt from my brother's suicide is the ignorance of people towards suicide. People do not want to discuss suicide, perhaps because of societal stigma, or maybe it is not worthy of discussion. Parents can talk about sex and relationships, but not suicide. People think it is outrageous for someone to commit suicide, but the same people can justify why they should take someone's life. In many societies committing suicide is a taboo. When your nuclear family member commits suicide people look at you differently. The stigma affects relationships. It divides families. People think it is a hereditary cause, so they think you may be the next victim in your family. You see your extended family detaching themselves from you and your nuclear

CHUKWUMA JULIUS OKONKWO

family because they do not want to be part of the cause. The ignorance blinds people from seeing suicide for what it really is, and that is that it is a natural phenomenon that needs to be discussed all the time for us to understand how to help people who are at the risk of suicide. Many people do not understand that a decision to commit suicide takes time. This is because the victim has to process the thoughts of committing suicide, then look for the means to commit suicide, and wait for the opportunity to come. Sometimes the loved ones are the people who provide the means and opportunities to commit suicide. We do not realize that our actions or inactions can push someone into committing suicide. We do not realize that the negative things we say to people who are prone to suicide can torture their minds and compel them to end their life. We are ignorant because we do not discuss suicide. We only talk about suicide as a gossip.

Imagine you have a mental disorder that nobody understands, except you. You have family and friends who remind you all the time how difficult it is for them to cope with your mental illness. Sometimes they do not tell you directly to your face, but you see it through their actions towards you and you hear it from other people. When you do something wrong you are asked if your mental issues have come back again. They think you are putting much pressure on them. Then you are shipped to a psychiatrist hospital where you are maltreated. Because it is in your nature to resist maltreatment the staffs chain and torture you and then claim that you are violent. Nobody, including your family and friends, believes what you say about how you are maltreated by the hospital staffs because whenever you talk people think it is a mad person talking. You still think about your dreams and you want to pursue your dreams. But, your dreams are all tied to the chains in your hands and legs. Because no one believes what you say, you store everything in your heart until your heart becomes so big that it cannot contain your thoughts anymore. You want to write, but your hands are chained. You want to talk, but there is no listening ear. You want to run away, but your legs are chained. You need the freedom to pursue your dreams. The hospital is making you really mad. You cannot break the chains. The only option is to use your mind as a weapon. So, you decide to play cool and nice. When you are abused at the hospital you accept it so that you are not labelled violent.

Few months later they think you are fine and everything is okay with you. They do not know that your heart is full and waiting to explode like a time bomb. Then they grant you freedom to go home. But, there is no home for you because the place you call home is full of people who do not understand you, people who do not believe you, people who allowed you to be chained like a violent mad person even when you do not deserve that, and people who see you as a liability. You do not want to be anybody's liability or responsibility. You just want to live your life. But, you cannot because of the people around you. You do not want to be shipped to a psychiatrist hospital anymore to be chained and tortured by staffs. You cannot live with people who do not believe what you say. You think you have lost their trust and they have lost yours too. Even though your family tells you that they love you, you do not see the love in their words. With your heart heavy and no one to confide in the only thing in your mind is to go to somewhere you can find freedom and that is to take the unconventional path to death. At that point the only thing that makes sense to you is death. If someone starts telling you how beautiful life is that will be a waste of your time and will not make you change your mind. What can make you change your mind is someone who is confident to talk about what you have in mind and what makes your heart heavy at that point. If you get a sense that someone can endure what you are going through, that someone has gone through what you are going through and still lives, and that someone has another solution other than the one (death) you have in mind, perhaps you will listen and change your mind.

If you can imagine yourself in that scenario, then you will get a sense of what people who are at the risk of suicide go through. Now you have an understanding of how you can engage with someone who is about to commit suicide. Most times it is convenient for us to remind people who are about to commit suicide of how beautiful life is, but they already know. Though, it is not that simple. Sometimes they need to be reminded of how beautiful life is, however, sometimes reminding of the beautiful things in life could be a trigger. But, in most cases

CHUKWUMA JULIUS OKONKWO

what they need is a reassurance that they are not alone in that situation they have found themselves. They need genuine options other than the option of death that they have in mind. People who consider suicide as an option are broken on the inside. Sometimes when we see people who are broken by the challenges that they face in life, we do not really understand how seriously broken they are on the inside that a mere reminder of how beautiful life is cannot fix them. We cannot always fix people who are inwardly broken, even though we often think we can. Only them can fix themselves. But it is not as simple as it sounds. All they need is someone who can genuinely tell them that they can make things right because some people have been in their shoes and made things right, someone they can look in the eyes and see the truth, and a comforting shoulder to lay their heads on. Unfortunately, we often try to force ourselves into fixing them. Then we, eventually, end up slitting them deeper with the fragments from their broken selves. We should change our perception about suicide and victims of suicide. We should talk about suicide often because that is the way we can understand suicide and the pangs that people who consider suicide as an option go through, and help those who are prone to suicide. That is how we can save people from committing suicide.

CHAPTER 13

The Parable of the Blind Bartimaeus

BARTIMAEUS WAS THE blind son of Timaeus. He was not only blind, but was also a street beggar. Jesus restored his sight. But, before Jesus restored his sight something sterling and motivating happened. Jesus had been performing miracles and healings before that day, so the miracle on Bartimaeus was not his first miracle or healing. Here is the parable of the blind Bartimaeus. Jesus was in the city of Jericho with his disciples for his divine works. As they were leaving, Bartimaeus was sitting by the road begging, as usual. Then he heard that it was Jesus, he started shouting, "Jesus, Son of David, have mercy on me!" Although, many people censured him and tried to shut him up, he refused to be shut up and continued to shout, "Jesus, Son of David, have mercy on me!" Consequently, his shouting caught Jesus' attention and he asked for Bartimaeus to be called. Jesus asked him what he would want him to do for him, and Bartimaeus replied that he would want to be able to see again. Thus, Jesus told him to go home that his faith had set him free. In a blink of an eye, Bartimaeus gained his sight back. That was the miraculous healing that restored Bartimaeus' sight.

You may be wondering what the parable of the blind Bartimaeus has to do with you. It has everything to do with you. There are many moral lessons to learn from that parable. I previously mentioned that before Jesus restored Bartimaeus sight that something sterling and motivating happened, remember? What happened was the persistence of Bartimaeus despite all the scorns from people to shut up. That persistence was a reflection of two things. One was the power of faith and the other was the power of focus. With his persistent shouting for

Jesus to save him, Bartimaeus revealed not just an uncommon faith in the power of Jesus to restore his sight, but also a stern focus on what he wanted from Jesus. Remember that Jesus asked him what he wanted from him and he went straight to the point that he wanted his sight back.

Many people do not know what they want in life. This is why when they are presented with an opportunity to say what they want or how they would want to be helped, they simply wobble. Life does not only present you with challenges, it also presents you with opportunities to deal with your challenges. Knowing what you want helps you to utilize opportunities when they come your way. You need to have the power of focus that Bartimaeus had in order to be able to utilize the opportunities that come your way in life. Any opportunity that you miss at any point in your life may not come back again. This is because opportunities do not repeat themselves. The power of focus enables you to prioritize your challenges by narrowing them down to specifics. Indeed, life presents us with many challenges that we cannot deal with at the same time. But, by prioritizing your challenges you will understand better the challenges that are most pressing and as such demand the most attention. Then you will focus efforts towards tackling them.

Opportunities do not send notices, rather they happen by chance. That is why they are called opportunities. What this means is that you have to be ready at any time to take advantage of the opportunities that life presents to you. Bartimaeus did not have any prior notice that Jesus was in Jericho. He just happened to be begging by the roadside, as usual, when Jesus and his disciples were leaving the city. He had been blind for too long and had wanted to see again. That was not his only challenges; he was very poor and as such had resorted to street begging as a means of survival. But, getting his sight back was his pressing problem. He could have asked Jesus to give him wealth instead of his sight, or he could have tried to outline all his problems to Jesus when he asked him what he wanted from him. But he did not; rather he focused on his pressing problem. Imagine if he had missed that opportunity. Imagine if Bartimaeus had wobbled. He might not have had the opportunity to meet Jesus again, and he would have remained blind for the rest of his life. Just like Bartimaeus you need to be strategic about prioritizing your challenges. Many people are looking for help, but when you ask them how you can help them they are often not able to give you a clear answer. You must have clarity in your responses when you are confronted with such a question. Indeed, it may be tempting to frontload all your problems to someone, who is willing to assist you. That is certainly not a smart move. You may scare the person away with your litany of problems. Nobody can help you with all your problems. Develop a mind-set that life is one step at a time. That will help you to focus attention on the things that matter the most.

The power of focus as exemplified by Bartimaeus was a reflection of his determination to receive his sight back. Imagine the blindness that was referred to in the parable of the blind Bartimaeus as obstacles that have prevented you from achieving those life goals you have set to achieve. Imagine the blindness as challenges that have made impossible your efforts to move to the next level in your career. Imagine the blindness in the context of your situation in your family or school or workplace. Imagine the blindness as something that has obstructed you from moving ahead like your counterparts. Imagine the blindness as something you desire the most in your life. Many people want something but not everyone has the determination to get what they want. Whichever way you have imagined the blindness to reflect your circumstances you must realize that determination is the watchword. You have to be determined to put in hard work in order to get the positive result that you want to see. Determination means not giving up when you are told to give up, it means not shutting up when you are being scorned and asked to shut up, it means not surrendering to pressure when you are pressured to surrender or confronted with many challenges at the same time. Rather determination means understanding that every effort you put into something will not always produce a 'yes' response, it means understanding that you do not stop doing what you are doing because you have received so many 'no' responses, it means that you do not succumb to people's opinions, and it means being persistent and hopeful like the symbolic phoenix and ready to rise from the ashes of your struggles. Imagine if Bartimaeus had listened to what many people told him and shut up. Obviously, Jesus would have left the city of Jericho without noticing him. And Bartimaeus would have remained blind for the rest of his life. Sometimes you need to shout for you to be heard. You need to be persistent when you are seeking for help. Your persistence shows how seriously you want something. People will not take you seriously if you do not show them how serious you are. Your loud cry may signal your seriousness, hard work and determination to getting the help that you seek.

Most times we often brand others the cause of our blindness without looking inwards into ourselves. If you want to solve a problem you must start from the real cause of the problem. When you blame others for your problem you may never find a solution to your problem. There is a Nigerian (Igbo) adage loosely translated into English which says that, pollution in the river starts from the source and then spreads. This suggests that your problems in life have a source and from that source they multiply and spread. The only person that deserves to be blamed for your problems is you. You are the source of your problems. This is a difficult thing to accept. Putting the blame upon yourself is accepting responsibility for whatever happens to your life and that helps you to find solutions to your problems. In whatever way the blindness in the parable resonates with you, you must see yourself as responsible for your blindness. Perhaps if Bartimaeus had blamed his father or mother or somebody else for causing his blindness he might not have taken the pain to stay by the roadside crying loud to Jesus to save him. This is because putting blame on other people for what you are going through in life does not allow you to think of ways you can solve your problems. It creates a fertile ground for dependence. It rather makes you too dependent on those people because you think they owe you the solution. You must realize that the solutions to your problems lie in your hands. This is why you must always strive with hard work and determination in every situation you find yourself in life.

In whatever way the parable of the blind Bartimaeus resonates with you, let the powers of faith and focus that Bartimaeus exemplified inspire you. You remain in your blindness because you have lost faith in who you are and what you can do. If you do not have faith in yourself nobody is going to have faith in you. Bartimaeus' faith revealed his determination to getting his sight back. You should let your faith guide your hard work and determination. If you want someone to help you with, say money for your education or business, and you are not showing how determined you are to studying hard or pushing your business forward you are definitely not going to receive any help. Lacking faith and focus in the face of your blindness is simply prolonging the duration of your blindness. You prolong the duration of your blindness when you lose faith and focus on what you want. If you do not know what you want it will be hard for you to receive help from people. As you have seen already, what actually gave Bartimaeus his sight back were his faith and focus. He had his sight; then he was blind; and Jesus restored it with his faith and focus at the centre. Though he needed help from Jesus, but he helped himself in a most significant way with his faith and focus. This means that when you are seeking for help you have to help yourself by making it easier for people to help you. Clarity of focus is really important. Therefore, you need at all times to focus on what is most important. That will help you not to be distracted by the things that are less important. You must have greater level of faith to keep your focus in check.

CHAPTER 14

The Struggle of Being Black

A N ATTEMPT TO have a discussion about the term black always verges on opening a can of worms. This is because there are multiple conceptions about the term black. This often results to misconceptions about the term black and what it means to be black. I know a black guy who thinks that the virtue of him being a black person gives him the natural knowledge of understanding what the term black entails. I know a white pundit who thinks that his epistemic erudition has elevated him to the scholastic position to have an in-depth understanding of the term black and what it means to be black. Indeed, the term black, though it has become a locus classicus in today's world connotes something different to different people. It is often deliberately exploited to either aggrandize or belittle the pragmatics of a situation. Within that context of deliberate exploitation the term black is linked to a social construct and a political phrase, race. Indeed, black is a dynamic and complex term. Its understanding is naturally complicated. The different connotations of black have not been exhaustively investigated to persuade a clear understanding of what the term black really is. Thus, it will be impossible to claim knowledge of what it means to be black, even when you have experienced it first-hand. I can only make a modest attempt to write about being black based on my experience as a black man. My experiences are encapsulated in my struggles. Being black is a struggle.

Being black is a struggle only the black people can resonate and really identify with, based on their experience. For me, this struggle comes from the suffix, 'ness', attached to the word black. Put together, blackness makes being black a struggle. There is no single way to define blackness. The suffix, 'ness', comes from the colour allegory that is often used to describe black. This description dates back to centuries ago, and has since continued to exist up to the present day. The description also has undertones of race. If you are described as black, you are a product of a certain region of the world and you are treated as such. With this description comes a belief – the belief that dark colouration of the skin defines black, therefore, dark skin colour represents black. If you and I are dark-skinned, then we are categorised as the same, otherwise we are different. The belief informs perceptions – the perceptions that people have of themselves and other people; the perceptions that influence people's state of mind and identity based on their skin colour. Because we are dark-skinned, therefore, we must align ourselves as one people and interact only amongst ourselves. Thus, with the suffix, 'ness', comes the conditions, beliefs, perceptions, mind-sets and identities that characterize black. With these elements blackness creates loads – which can be psychological, social, economic, cultural or political – that every black person carries, but differently. These loads are struggles of being black. The struggles shape the experiences of the black people. And these experiences are the lessons of and for the black people.

Although, life is full of struggles, however, the struggles that being black bring, especially living in a world that is full of racism and intolerance of all kinds, outweigh all the struggles of life. Indeed, people who oppose what has appeared to be a movement, 'black lives matter', and introduce what has also appeared to be another set of movement, 'all lives matter', are invited to oppose this view. It is only when you eat the African cherry fruit (udara) that you will be able to say how sweet or sour it tastes in the mouth. The struggles of being black are real. Though, these struggles resonate well with black people, however, it does not suggest that all black people identify with these struggles because some black people, for some ulterior reasons, live in denial of their struggles. This is why you see some black people deny that racism is non-existent.

For me, the struggle of being black starts from childhood. It makes you inquisitive because you want to know everything about your heritage. It does not matter the country you are raised in. The hunger to learn about your heritage is not restricted to any boundaries or geographical locations. You always ask questions, you always search for answers, and you always look for clarity. But, as a black kid you are faced with different versions of your heritage, from what your parents tell you (if they happen to be open about it), to what your teachers teach you in school, and to the (single) narratives given in the mainstream media. You may find it really hard to reconcile these different versions of narratives. In doing that, sometimes you may be tempted to doubt your heritage depending on how persuasive the distortions you are sold are. If you are quite exposed to resources by your parents, you will read books, watch documentaries and hear stories about black histories. Sometimes, the pages of the books or the screens of the television may turn into wounds, because you have read or seen how unbalanced the world is, how far away the ideal world you have in your head is from the real world you live in, and how impossible it is to undo the injustices that have been done, you cannot help, but let the passion to do things differently burn into your heart. Then the older you get the more struggles you face; they come, like mosaics, in different forms and shades, and you learn from your experience or experience of others to deal with every struggle that you face. However, coping with your struggles is not like attending a friend's free dinner party; rather it requires you to dance in the rain. Sometimes you may be left out in the cold, while you are dancing in the rain.

In 2013, I wrote a poem titled, 'Struggle of a black child', and then a white pen friend told me that she read it and felt enthusiastic about being black in her next life. I raised my antenna and wondered why she would want to be black; I could not understand why she would wish to throw away all her white privileges, just to become black. For me, her wish equates someone wanting to leave the sight of an eagle masquerade dancing to go and watch an act of exorcism. An eagle masquerade is a prestigious traditional masquerade of the Igbo people in Nigeria that is used as a form of entertainment. You can imagine someone choosing to watch where somebody is being delivered from evil spirit rather than enjoying the dance of the prestigious eagle masquerade. When I picked her brain further on her wish, it became clear to me, from her response, that her enthusiasm about wanting to be black was not because she was touched by the emotions that run through the stanzas of the poem, she was rather being sarcastic. She happened to be one of those people who often live in denial of white privileges. Engage them in a discussion and they will hide under the cover of social construction to give you litany of (defensive) reasons why white privileges do not exit. These days the easiest way to defend a punch in a debate is to label the concept a socially constructed concept that needs to be deconstructed.

It is really hard to understand what it means to be black if you are not black. This is the same way it is hard to understand the cultural loads that an Aboriginal and Torres Strait Islander in Australia carries, or the intergenerational grief that someone from the south-east of Nigeria carries from the tragedy of Biafra war, if you are not part of that community of people. It is only a black woman that knows the struggle of being challenged to alter her natural dark skin to manufacture an artificial skin that looks nothing closer to a white skin. It is only a black youth in the United Kingdom (UK) that knows how stop-and-search perpetuated by the UK police feels like. It is only a black teenager in Australia that understands what it feels like to be labelled a gang member and potentially dangerous based on his or her physical appearance. It is only a black person in the United States of America (USA) that understands what it feels like to deal with being discriminated against by the institutions of the state, possibly all his or her entire life, based on his or her dark-skinned colour. The struggles are real, but you will not understand until you walk in the shoes of a black person.

Now let me speak to some people. Imagine you are a little black teenager, you live in a white dominated society, you are a responsible kid and so are your friends. Every time you walk down the street you are confronted by white teenagers who have been indoctrinated, by their parents, into the thinking that their white skin colour represents superiority. Then you are bullied, but you never buckle under their intimidation, you always fight back because that is what your parents have taught you. At the white-dominated school you and your friends attend, your teachers often think that you and your friends are always up to something bad, perhaps because of the bad things they read in the mainstream media. So, each time they see you and your friends they develop a mental image of potential gangsters, then you become a screen that other white teens in your school stare at every time you walk pass by, and when you try to come within a few feet of their space, perhaps to play with them, you are confronted with such looks of fear in their faces. If you walk into a grocery shop, the shopkeeper develops a pictorial sense of a shoplifter and takes over-the-top safety measures to ensure safety of items in the shop, sometimes you are told instantly that you cannot afford the items that you intend to buy, so you should back off. For you, the only place that you have never received untoward treatment and that nobody sees you through the colour of your skin is in your local church. You have been taught to always be tolerant whenever you are in public, so each time you feel that your presence makes other people jumpy you will divorce yourself from their sight until you feel that you have dissipated the pressure. But, you keep asking yourself for how long will that continue?

Indeed, the struggles come with sacrifices, compromises, and even denials. Personally, having travelled and lived in different white dominated countries that have recurring racism, I have been presented with difficult situations where the only option was to sacrifice my wants just to be part of the circle with my white friends, or to compromise my principles to avoid making them jumpy in public, or to even deny that an act of racial discrimination happened just to avoid being seen as overreacting. These may not resonate with you as struggles, but you have to wait until you become the man who does not appreciate the pains of childbirth that women experience until he experiences a worst case of constipation. You need to be black to be able to understand how to cope in public when your kindness to white people is interpreted as a strange act, or your precaution to be silent in some situations is seen as secretly planning to do something dangerous, or your dialect is often described as a slang, or your accent is depicted as crude, or your fluency in English language is described as extraordinary feat, or your unique culture is depicted as primitive and eerie, or your confidence is called arrogance. You must be black to understand the pain of working or studying where your mistakes are counted as incompetence, or your outstanding performance in a team or class group is described as a mere luck, or your ability to challenge ideas means being aggressive, or your response to personal attacks is interpreted as being violent, or your speaking up against harassment means being too over-reactive, or your ability to ask questions means you are unintelligent.

There is no single recipe for dealing with the struggles that blackness presents. If you are looking for an answer to how to deal with your struggles the answer to your quest is that the answer is elusive. You just have to deal with them in your own way. But, you have to make yourself less distressing. It takes an exceptional character for people to give up their own lives to contain the treatments they receive from other people. That is the struggle of being black.

CHAPTER 15

What is Your Bottom Line?

YOU MAY HAVE heard the term bottom line used in board meetings, or financial transactions, or business discussions, or general conversations. But, it is seems to be popular in boardroom meetings, when companies discuss their overall earnings. Then you hear question, like 'how will this affect the bottom line?' Few years ago, precisely in 2014, I was on my way to work, and then I still had my research position job in Nigeria. By the roadside were two grown men, perhaps in their mid-30s, arguing. The argument was intense and loud, so it was not difficult to know what the bone of contention was. One had bashed the other's car, but the dent was not too bad. In the course of the argument I overheard the guy whose car was bashed use the term bottom line to emphasize the point that, at minimum, the other guy would repair the damage to his car. Before then I had not heard the term in a while, so it triggered my antenna, something struck my curious mind to think about the term bottom line in another context. You would definitely be right if you said that I think about life too much. I think about life in different contexts, that is how I get insights and clarity about things in life. Thus, I thought about bottom line in a bigger context of everyday life.

When people talk about bottom line, regardless of the context, they refer to something important and a minimum level. Thus, in the context of life, your bottom line can be something that is most important that you cannot trade for anything, or a minimum level of something that you can compromise or tolerate. It is something that you need to figure out yourself. Permit me to provoke some questions in your mind now. Basically, I will try to make you understand this term in the context of everyday life you live. Think for a second about these questions: What is the most important thing that defines your life that you cannot trade for anything? If you have to compromise something, what is the minimum compromise that you can make for or accept from others? If you have to accommodate people in your life, what fraction of space can you give up, at minimum, for them? If you have to tolerate people's attitude, what is your minimum level of tolerance? What is the minimum level of pity that you can accept from others? Litany of these questions can continue inexhaustibly. These questions are relevant for two reasons. One is that there are many events in life that can cause a shift in reality of life. Things can change unexpectedly and people you may know very well can change to the point that you do not know them anymore. Two is that they can help you in understanding why you have continued to face the challenges that you face in life – be it marital or relationship or educational or business or career challenges. As you think about the challenges that you face, ask yourself, what is your bottom line? As you ponder over events in your life, ask yourself, what is your bottom line?

I remember a tragic incident that happened in Nigeria in 2014. The Nigerian Immigration Service was recruiting and had invited thousands of unemployed youths to sit for aptitude tests. The number of candidates was far higher than the venue could contain. Then there was a stampede, the unfortunate incident happened, and many people died while many sustained injuries. There was a public outcry that went on for weeks, as the families of the victims licked their wounds from the painful incident. No doubts, the Immigration Service was responsible for the deaths and injuries of those candidates. How about the candidates themselves? What if their impatience had not led them to the commotion that caused the stampede? What if they had defined that most significant element that they would not compromise, it could be their self-worth? What if they had all valued their lives that they would not trade life for anything? What if the pregnant woman, who died with her baby during the stampede had defined that her baby was the most important element in her life that she would not trade for anything, including the aptitude test? What if the candidates had defined the minimum condition they would allow anyone to subject them to; they could have refused to take the aptitude test in such a condition? What if they had realized the power of choice in their hands and made the decision not to write the aptitude test in that deplorable condition and reported the situation? What if they had normalized the tempo of their extreme anxiety to get a federal government job? Would there have been a stampede? Perhaps they would have been alive.

It is often popular among people to take short-cuts. Taking short-cuts does not allow you the opportunity to make informed decisions. There is no short-cut when you define your bottom line. Your bottom line reminds you that in every situation you have a choice to make, and guides you in making that choice. You have the power of choice in your hands to decide what you want in life and the people you want in your life. Your bottom line helps you to decide how you want to be treated by others. I met a girl in Australia, who was always battered by her boyfriend. When I asked her why she was still with him, she could not give any reason, except that she loved him. I said to myself, "what a stupid answer, really?" What if she had created a bottom line that defined what behaviour that she would not tolerate from her boyfriend? Obviously, she would not have allowed herself to be beaten a second time, not repeatedly. When you do not have a bottom line you get caught up in situations that you cannot easily get out of. But, there is no situation you cannot get out of, if you decide strongly to work towards getting out. Life comes with a purpose. Your bottom line helps you to define that purpose. Therefore, every life should have a bottom line. I would argue that any life that is devoid of bottom line is not worth living. This is because every situation you find yourself in will seem like a Rubicon. I have a bottom line that tells me what I can tolerate and what I cannot tolerate. You cannot quantify bottom line in monetary terms, unfortunately. Underneath my field of vision lies my bottom line. Where is your bottom line?

There is no limit to how many bottom lines you can create for yourself, in case you wonder if it is just a one thing. Your bottom line should apply to every aspect of your life, because in life you deal with all kinds of challenges and people. If you understand that life is a stage and that every stage in life comes with challenges that present you with choices to make, then you will understand how important it is that you create something that helps you to remember that power of choice and make those choices. This is what bottom line does. The choices that we make in life determine our experience and vice versa. If you have friends who undermine your abilities, you have a choice to leave that circle of friends. You cannot allow yourself to be treated like that. If you come from a family where nobody respects your wish to carve your own niche, you have a choice to reject their opinions and follow your dream. When you become successful they will remember you share the same surname with them and then they will tell you how proud they are of you. If you are in a relationship that brings you more pain than happiness, you have a choice to quit the relationship. It is not a life time covenant, you deserve to be happy.

Imagine your life is a mosaic with a collection of colours. Every canvas does not depict a rainbow, but contains a hue of other colours. If you do not like the paintings depicted on the canvas of your life (the mosaic), you have a choice, either to take a painting brush and turn the mosaic (your life) into a masterpiece that you desire, or watch other people paint their masterpiece while you sit and complain. Your challenge in life is like a card that life deals you on the table. Whatever drawing that is on the card you have on you is a reflection of your challenges. If you turn over the card and you do not like the drawing on the card, you have a choice to change the drawing on the card to reflect what you want. That choice is either to embrace your challenges and deal with them or complain and become a loser in life. You cannot sit and wait for the card to change into a drawing of your choice or for someone to turn your mosaic into a masterpiece that you desire. This means that you cannot wish away the challenges that life presents you with. It is either you deal with your problems or your problems will continue to deal with you.

Your life is too precious to be surrounded by people who do not respect you. People disrespect you because you gave them the reason to disrespect you. By sticking around them each time you are disrespected you are telling them that you are worthless. Because you have shown them how worthless you are they take pride in disrespecting you. They believe that no matter how bad they treat you, you will still stick around. Imagine you are a woman and a guy inappropriately taps your butt, and you say nothing. Next time the guy will do it again. As long as you continue to maintain your silence each time the guy taps your butt he will continue to do it. Another guy, who notices your silence, might want to tap your butt too. Before you know it every guy in the hood taps your butt. That is because you have given them the mandate to tap your butt with your silence. Your bottom line enables you to examine your life to make choices about who stays in or leaves your life, and how people should treat you. When you create a bottom line you will stop accepting disrespect from other people. Your dignity, honour and respect are not negotiable. You must always protect them otherwise people will always take you for granted and think that it is okay to disrespect you.

The world is full of insincerity. Insincerity has become a currency that most people spend to get what they want from other people. These days people tell you what you want to hear to get what they want from you. I learnt a lot from my late father's life. His life experiences taught me that in life there are many people who pretend to be who they are not or pretend not to be who they are. These are snakes in human skin; they hide under the grass, perhaps the grass you created. While the snakes are personification of sycophants you allow into your life, the grass is a personification of the incentives that you create that draw those sycophants close to you. They are always around you, like parasites. Parasites cannot live without hosts because they feed on their hosts. Because everything is working out well for you, your life is succulent, that's why they stick around you. However, you are relevant to them until you run out of those nutrients that attract them. They preach their loyalty to you until your situation goes bad, their loyalty ends, and then you realize that loyalty is like a commodity; it can be bought and sold and often it goes to the highest bidder. Put their loyalty in check and they will reveal their true colour.

My late father created the grass on which snakes in the form of family and friends thrived. He did not realize how tall he had allowed the grass to grow and as such how many snakes he had given comfortable homes until he became really sick and was bedridden. No doubts, you will definitely have such snakes in your life. This is why you have to always keep the grass low. Your bottom line will help you to keep the grass in your life low. Can you imagine what happens when the grass is always low? Obviously, all the snakes will have no hiding place, they will all be exposed, and you will always see their true colour. Letting the grass to grow tall will only help to conceal the snakes and provide them with comfortable homes. The snakes come and take over your grass at your expense. You just have to make a choice. You cannot keep letting people come into your life and mess your life up. You cannot keep giving people free access to your emotions when they do not deserve to have a place in your life. You cannot keep passing balls to people who do not deserve a shot on goal. You cannot keep seeking for other people's validation when you are the captain of your life and have the power of choice in your hand. Life is like a boat ride; not everyone is needed on the boat. You only need a limited number of people on the boat. The fewer the people on your boat are, the merrier and easier your ride will become. But, when your boat is filled with many people, it is most likely to sink, and your boat ride will end up a bummer. Your life comes with a purpose. You should have a bottom line. Find your purpose in life, define your bottom line, and let your bottom line guide and inform your choices.

CHAPTER 16

Why Are We Always Judgmental?

I MAGINE YOU ARE a male and in a restaurant having your dinner, you notice a girl sitting alone, she is chewing a gum, then your eyes meet, she smiles and winks at you, you respond with a hand sign that invites her to your table, she stands up, now you see the way she is dressed, from afar you see her inviting cleavages and the oval-shaped body she is showcasing, and while she walks she smiles and winks at some other guys. All of a sudden she is sitting in front of you. It is Friday, the evening is going too fast, so you go straight to the point and ask her how much for the night. She gets angry, snarls at you and walks away. Now you realize that she is not who you thought she was. You think that, from the way she is dressed and is overly smiling and winking, she may be a hooker. Then you feel sorry for yourself because you know you should not have judged her. But, because you did, you jumped into conclusion of who you thought she was.

Imagine you are a teacher and there is a boy in your class who always comes to class late. You have never bothered to find out why he is always late. You conclude that he is lazy to wake up early, like most students, to prepare for class. Whenever he comes in late you will punish him, sometimes you will humiliate him in front of the class, and while you punish him you always tell him of how great your children, who are younger than he is, are at waking themselves up early and getting ready for school. But, that will not change anything, as he continues to come late to class. One day you deliberately fixed a class test to hold very early in the morning. You know that based on his unbeatable records as a latecomer there is no way he will make the test. You have a rule that absence in the test means repeating the class. You could care less if he failed. On the day of the test, you are walking down the street, quite early in the morning, after your morning jog. Suddenly, an accident happens, right in front of you, someone riding a bicycle has been knocked down by a vehicle, in a blink of an eye it has become an accident scene. Then you see a familiar face; it is the boy in your class, he is the victim. He has been beating the traffic lights, unlike him, because he wants to finish his morning deliveries early so that he will not miss the class test. But, he met the devil on that last traffic light and the devil could not let him go free.

The bicycle he was riding is his delivery bicycle; he has a delivery job where he delivers all kinds of things, including the newspapers that you read every morning while you go to work. That is what he does every morning before he goes to school, and he takes care of himself and his younger sister from the money that he earns from his delivery job. Now you remember all the punishments you have given him and all the humiliations in class, and then you realize that he is not actually a lazy boy who cannot wake up early to prepare for school, as you thought; he is a complete opposite of what you thought. Then you wish you had not judged him and drawn your conclusions. You wish you had asked him earlier why he was always late in class. You feel really bad. But, the accident has happened, he is the victim with many injuries, and you cannot change what has happened.

Some will argue that making judgments about people is different from being judgmental. By differentiating the two, you feel it is more convenient and acceptable to make judgments than being judgmental. Therefore, making judgments becomes a diluted version of being judgmental, where people who are judgmental hide under the cover of making judgments. In general sense, the word judgmental in the dictionary connotes two meanings. On one hand, being judgmental deals with making judgments. You see, at the fundamental level of semantic, making judgments is (equally) being judgmental. It does not matter whether your judgment is good or bad. You judge people for who they are or who you think they are. On the other hand, making judgements deals with being excessively critical, particularly in an unconstructive manner. You judge people based on who you think they should be or what you think they should do or should have done or how you think they should do or should have done things. Though these meanings present a semantic issue, for example, whether it is really judgmental when you are making good judgments about people, however, they persuade a conviction that a thin line exists between making judgments and being judgmental. Understanding this will help you to strike at the heart of this semantic issue. Oftentimes we are faced with the difficulty of how to make constructive judgments, which we may refer to as good judgments, relative to unconstructive judgments, which we may refer to as bad judgments and the problematic ones.

Now the big question is why are people judgmental? Most times people are judgmental because they do not understand what they are judging. If you know much about people you judge it is certain that you will be less likely to judge them. Sometimes people think that being judgmental helps them to understand other people better. Judging starts from creating images of how things should be. These may involve images of who you are, or who people are, or what you think, or what people are, or how people should be. Creating such images comes with assumptions about things or people. When you make assumptions about people they are enclosed in the images that you have created. These images are reflected through a lens, which is a mechanism through which you view things or perceive people and reinforce your judgments. This lens is idiosyncratic to you because it is personal to you and you use it to evaluate things or people. As human beings we are accustomed to habits, we like to do things repeatedly. So, most times when we create those images, with the assumptions, we sustain them by reinforcing them, and our habitual lifestyle as human beings helps us with that. This is why we often categorize people or situations as the same and treat them as such.

Also, people are judgmental because it is in human nature to judge. It seems sometimes like a reflex action that is built into our DNA and that we cannot control. This is because when we create those images, with the assumptions, we become instinctively connected to them, and being habitual human beings we do not want to change something that comes quite handy. Thus instantaneity becomes our preferred mode of operation, because we want to respond to situations or people as quickly as we can. Then with our idiosyncratic evaluative lens we make quick judgments about things or people. Thus, those judgments are often driven by force of power that make them empty of empathy because they are self-centered on our point of view, they are often unconstructive, which makes them problematic to deal with, and they are often excessively based on our perception of other people's behaviours. However, we can control, and even stop, our inclination to being judgmental. How can you do that?

It is easier to judge people than understand them. Judging people erodes your ability to understand them. This means that being judgmental does not and will not help you to understand people better. This is why it is crucial that you understand that the image that you have created in your mind, with the assumptions, whether they are about you or other people, are all yours alone and should not apply to other people. What this means is that you have to understand where the person you are judging has been to, that is what the person has experienced in life and the experiences that inform the person's choices and where the person is coming from, that is the perspective of the person you are judging. You have to understand the (hi)story behind the person's actions or inactions. We know that there are circumstances that are beyond our control, but we do not apply that knowledge to other people's case. We judge them like we know all their (hi)stories, and when we find out how wrong the little we know about them are we end up being sorry and ashamed, sometimes it is too late that we cannot change what we have done or remedy the damage that we have caused.

Though it may seem that judging people is such a reflex action that you can hardly control, but when you open up your mind to allow people to be the judge of themselves you will see that judging people only seems to be reflexive because you created the convenience that makes it a reflex action. The convenience lies in your habitual need to reinforce your judgments through your evaluative lens. Therefore, you have to be aware of the assumptions that are contained in the images that your evaluative lens is projecting. You form the assumptions based on the values that appeal to you. Those are your personal values and should be seen as such because other people have values that appeal to them which may be different from yours. As human beings we all have different frames that shape our values, where you received your values may not be the same as where other people received their values. This is what I call value-frame. Thus, you have to be aware of whose values are behind your evaluative lens. When you are about to judge someone, perhaps based on their choices, you should ask yourself whose value-frame you are proclaiming. Being aware of these things will help you to understand the direct and potential consequences of your judgments, particularly when your judgments carry much influence on other people, so that you can be aware of them. If you were the teacher that was referred to in the second story, obviously you did not realize your influence over the boy in your class until he was involved in that accident. If you were not being judgmental, you would not have fixed the class test that early, then the boy would not have tried to beat the traffic in order to finish his deliveries early to catch up with the class test, and the boy would not have been involved in that accident.

CHAPTER 17

You've Complained… Now What?

A S AN INQUISITIVE person, I have always been interested in understanding people. What I have observed through my interactions with people is that a lot of people like to complain. I know that psychologists have demonstrated why people complain and I understand and acknowledge that it is natural for us as human beings to express our dissatisfaction with something, however, what I do not endorse is people complaining all the time about something they somehow have control over. I understand that our situation varies – we face (or have faced) different things in life – but we should not let what we are facing (or have faced) obstruct the good things that are ahead of us. It is like letting the past or even the present obstruct the future. Let me be clear, I genuinely believe that people should express their feelings of dissatisfaction or disappointment, but what I am against is people dwelling so much on their dissatisfaction or disappointment that it prevents them from taking actions to undo what has been done. Expressing your feelings of discontent should be transient. When expressing how you feel about something goes beyond a moment, then it becomes a baggage.

When I interact with people and they complain about something my response is usually 'now what?' The retort, now what, is often to stimulate in the mind of the person I am interacting with that regardless of how ugly the situation emerges to be, there must be a follow-on action to undo whatever animated those feelings of disappointment. What this means is that you cannot just complain and do nothing afterwards. It is such a complete waste of time to complain about something all the time without doing anything to change what it is you always complain about. The world is not designed to be perfect; hence

CHUKWUMA JULIUS OKONKWO

human beings are not created to be perfect. The implication of these is that things do not (always) happen according to our wishes. And people do not (always) behave according to how we wish they would behave. As long as we continue to live on this planet there will always be situations that will bring disappointments and dissatisfactions. Therefore, constantly complaining about something is like someone playing aquatics complaining about being wet in water. If you do not want to get wet then you should not participate in aquatics. So, if you cannot do something about what you are complaining about then you should not complain at all.

I know that some complaints are quite justified, but, in general, too much complaining often leads to self-destruction. I have heard young people in certain parts of the world complain consistently about the old generation suffocating their opportunities to participate in nation building. I have heard graduates complain that they cannot find jobs because the old sets of politicians in their countries have ruined the economy; hence making it extremely hard for jobs to be created. I have heard people with good business ideas complain that they cannot find help with the seed money to kick-start their business because their parents or rich uncles or aunties that are well-connected in society are not willing to help them. I get it – your frustration and anger. But now what? Are you going to keep waiting for the opportunities to be handed over you, or are you going to be brave and mobilize people of like minds to create opportunities yourselves? You have got to decide whether you want to go hard or go home. You must understand that nothing will change about your complain unless you do something to change it. What is important is the action that you take to make the situation better. So, if you are sitting and complaining about being unemployed, for example, remember that there are many other unemployed people like you. Therefore, the difficulty in finding a job is not preserved to you. And what is at stake is not just your future, but also the future of many other unemployed people like you. I ask you again, now what? What are you going to do about it?

Today, we live in a world where relationship – marital or non-marital – failure is on the rise. I have seen couples, who spend time complaining about their marital problems and blaming others for being responsible for those problems, rather than taking actions to fix their marital problems. I have seen parents, who waste their energy complaining to others about their children's bad behaviours, rather than living up to their parental responsibilities. I have seen brothers and sisters, who are comfortable with complaining about their sibling's character flaw, rather than helping them to become better persons. I have seen friends, who spend time nit-picking each other's behaviour, rather than spending time to understand one another. So, when people complain to me about their relationships my response at the end of it all is 'now what'? You keep complaining or do something?

Now let me speak to some people. You are a woman, all the time you complain about your husband – his infidelity or alcohol problems or extravagance or parsimony or dishonesty. Now what? You can continue to complain and nothing will happen because your incessant complain is never going to change him, or you can understand that he needs help and take actions to help him, or you can summon the courage and walk away. You are a man, every time you complain about your wife's behaviour – she is a bad cook, or she is reckless with money, or she is naïve. Now what? You can either keep complaining or help her to become the better woman you want to see. You are a parent, you have complained about your child's truancy at school. Now what? Your brother or sister is a crack-head, I heard you clearly, but now what? Your parents were alcoholics or drug addicts and that was why your upbringing was dysfunctional. I get it. But, you are grown now. So what? Your parents got divorced or separated when you were very young and your mother and father were not there for you when you needed them. So you grew up with your grandparent without knowing your parents. All the time you complain that life would have been different and much better if your parents were in your life. I can image that feeling. But, are you not grown now to be the captain of your life? Now what? Your boss is such a tough nut to crack and because of him/her you hate your job. Now what? Keep complaining about your boss, or suck it up and figure out a way to get along with your boss? You have a large family and many friends, yet you feel like the loneliest person on earth because no one calls to check up on you. And because of that you are always sad and complaining. Now what? Are you going to keep complaining about that all your life, or face the cold hard truth that nobody owes you anything?

My interactions with people have made me to understand that many people do not understand that complaining about something all the time is nothing but a waste of time. Time is too precious to be wasted on complaining about things that you can change by taking actions. The amount of time that you spend complaining about your parent's or brother's or sister's addiction to drugs or alcohol and how their addiction has negatively impacted you is enough time to help them seek help and even seek your own help. You must accept the reality that your happiness resides with you and not with anybody else. This means that it is your responsibility to make yourself happy if happiness is what you want. I have not seen anyone become successful in their craft by complaining all the time. You must understand that complaining about something all the time has no place in the equation of success. This simply means that you cannot succeed in anything you have set out to do if all you do is complain. You cannot build strong and healthy relationships with others if you are always complaining because no one wants to be around a complainer. What complaining does to you is that it inspires you to blame others and sometimes puts you on the path of regret. By that you become comfortable with nit-picking; hence you end up living unhappy and unsatisfactory life. What can you achieve when you are always sad?

The fact of life is that no one wants to be around anyone who complains all the time, except you all are birds of a feather. This is because complaining brings negative vibes. Imagine that all your life you have been complaining about your parents – how their separation or divorce ruined your life, or how they failed to bequeath any inheritance to you, or how they failed to send you to college or university, or raise money for you to start your own business. Imagine that since you became an adult you have been complaining about how the old sets of politicians have ruined the economy of your country; hence all your adult life you have blamed the politicians for your economic hardships.

Imagine that all your marital life you have been blaming your partner for any problems in your marriage; hence for every hiccup in your marriage you have held your partner responsible for it. Imagine that in all your time in the corporate world you have blamed your colleagues or supervisors for every of your career somersault. You can imagine all the things you have been complaining about and blaming others for. What you have failed to realize in those years you have been complaining about those situations and blaming other people for your woes is your lack of self-awareness – of who you are as a person and your environment. I think that people who waste their time and energy complaining about something, rather than taking actions to undo what inspired what they are complaining about have zero self-awareness. What happens to you each time you dwell too much on expressing your dissatisfactions or disappointments is that your lack of self-awareness hides from you the ability to understand what you could do to turn around your situation.

You can relate whatever it is that you always complain about in your marriage or relationship or job to your lack of self-awareness. You must understand that the reason you are still complaining about your boss being a tough nut to crack, or your parents being drug or alcohol addicts, which has impacted your life, or your sibling being a gang member, which has brought shame to your family, or your partner being violent and abusive, which has pushed you into depression and so on, is that you are still not self-aware of your strengths, weaknesses, limitations, triggers and vulnerabilities. You still do not understand that relationship – whether marital or non-marital – is binary; it is either it works or it does not work. You are still not conscious of your personal values and preferences, and your natural inclinations. Above all, you still have not understood what being true to yourself means.

When I tell people that I do not complain, the philosophies behind it is that, one, I do not dwell too much on what has happened, rather I focus attention on how to salvage what has happened. Two, I have zero expectation of anything from anybody – parents, siblings, families and friends. These are the philosophies that have allowed me to nurture my self-awareness and deploy it at all times in my interactions with people. Because I have had too many bad experiences coupled with many disappointments, which have phenomenally fortified my mind-set, I tend to quickly snap out of my situations. However, it is hard to get people to understand that in my relationship with them that I do not expect or want anything because we live in a world where everyone believes that in a relationship everybody wants something. I think that the notion that everybody wants something is wrong and should not sound like a cliché. I think that the right notion should be that everybody needs something. I may need something from you in a relationship because I want to keep the relationship strong and alive. The concept of 'need' for me is that thing that is required to sustain the relationship. Thus without that 'need' relationship will die. But 'want' for me is an addition without which the relationship will still be strong and alive because we can live without what we want from each other. So from having an expectation we begin to want something; hence when what we expect and want is not there the relationship suffers. This is why I genuinely believe that we should all expect nothing from each other so that we will not want anything from each other. By that we will be able to build strong and lasting relationships.

CHAPTER 18

Being Fed vs Being Taught How To Hunt

WHEN I WAS a kid one of the lessons that I learnt from my parents, particularly my late father, was learning how to hunt for foods. My parents were sturdy believers in teaching a child how to hunt for foods as opposed to always feeding a child with foods. I grew up understanding that a boy of today will someday become a man and when that boy becomes a man the burden will be on him to provide for his family. Thus, the question that often confronted me as a growing kid was what would happen to a man who was fed all his life and was never taught how to hunt for foods? I remember asking my father that question as a kid and his response was simply that the man would die of hunger. As I grew older, that question continued to confront me. The fear of dying in penury made me a self-reliant kid. Thus, I grew up with the mind-set of hunting for foods and not waiting to be fed by someone.

There is a huge difference between being fed foods and being taught how to hunt for foods. The argument about being fed foods versus being taught how to hunt for foods draws attention to the concept of self-sufficiency. The argument about self-sufficiency is a long-standing one. Certainly, there is an incomplete knowledge about self-sufficiency. People's life experiences shape their understanding of what self-sufficiency means to them. While to some people self-sufficiency could come from being fed foods and at the same time being taught how to hunt for foods, however, to others self-sufficiency could come from not being fed at all but being taught how to hunt for foods from the outset. But what does it mean to be fed foods? And what does hunting for foods mean? To be fed foods is a figurative way of saying to be provided with something – for example, to be handed out or handed down something. To hunt for food is the opposite of being fed; hence, therefore, a figurative way of saying providing for yourself. Thus, food is a classic metaphor for what is handed out or handed down or provided or sought after. To be sure, these can be interpreted in different ways.

There is no magic bullet for self-sufficiency, but there are recipes for failure. One recipe for failure is not having the ability to hunt for food. In other words, dependence on other people for food is a recipe for failure. When you lack the ability to hunt for food, you will become dependent on others for food. Your dependency on other people for food does not only make you indolent and useless, but also puts you at a greater risk of meltdown when the economy collapses. If you are accustomed to the life of a recipient it will be extremely difficult for you survive when the economy nose-dives south. This is because you have nothing to leverage on. Depending on other people is like building a castle on a snow. Obviously, in chilled wintry weather the castle would survive as long as the snow remained iced. But, after the winter when the warm summer sun begins to shine the snow will melt away and the castle will collapse. In essence, dependence is an indication of a poor foundation for a purposeful and sustainable life.

Now let me speak to some people. Imagine that all your life you have been fed and all you know is how to eat. You have never hunted for food; hence you have depended on someone's hand-out to survive. If it is not your father, it is your mother. If it is not your brother, it is your sister. And if it is not your uncle, it is your aunty. Without your parents you are nobody and cannot exist. You cannot run a business without asking your parents for financial rescue. Your career progression is influenced by your last name and not by your performance. You are powered by other people; hence your entire life is connected to them as your power source. You are still breathing because your successful brother or sister is always your life support machine. Without those people whom your entire life is connected to for your survival you are dead. The question that you have got to ask yourself is what happens if those people whom your life is connected to as your power source stop to supply you power?

How are you going to give light to your life if those people who serve as your life support machines decide to pull the plug on you? Are you going to live in darkness the rest of your life because someone you have depended on your entire life decides to cut off his or her power supply? Think about these questions deeply!

Today, we live in a world where there is massive wave of sense of entitlement. The younger generations feel they are entitled to certain things from the older generations. Children feel they are entitled to certain things from their parents. Brothers and sisters feel they are entitled to certain things from their other siblings. A subordinate feels s/he is entitled to certain things from her/his boss. A colleague feels s/he is entitled to certain things from her/his co-workers. Friends feel they are entitled to certain things from you. Citizens feel they are entitled to certain things from the government. Politicians feel they are entitled to certain things from the electorates. In overall, everyone feels s/he is entitled to something. This sense of entitlement appears to be pronounced amongst the younger generations. Arguably, this is largely because most of the younger generations have been fed without being taught how to go into the world to hunt for foods. They are desirous of the finest things in life, yet they want those things to be delivered to them on a platter of gold. They believe that the world is designed to serve them. This is why a lot of young people live in the bubbles of idealism where they think that the world revolves around their thoughts and ideas. As a result of the way their mind-sets have been shaped to think that the world is ideal and all about them – their feelings, needs, wants, interests, preferences and choices – they tend to be obsessed with the end of everything and averse to the processes that lead to the end of that which they desire. This is why we see a lot of young people wishfully wanting to wear big boys' shoes, yet they do not want to go through the processes – which obviously are full of pains that must be endured – requisite of becoming a big boy.

However, I think, arguably, that the older generations are largely responsible for the entitlement complex that is common amongst the younger generations. This is premised on the way a lot of the older generations have raised their children by feeding them foods without

CHUKWUMA JULIUS OKONKWO

teaching them how to hunt for foods. I have heard many older generations say that they have worked so hard in their time to ensure that their children and generations to come will not have to suffer what they had suffered. In essence, they try to provide virtually everything for their children without teaching them how to hunt for foods. What happens is that the children will then grow up with a sense of entitlement that they deserve everything that they want, even when they haven't worked for anything. For me the failure of any parents to raise their children without teaching them how to hunt for foods is a clear indication of the children being spoilt. That also is setting the children up for failure. Odds are against any child who has been fed all his/her childhood and as such has grown into adulthood without learning how to hunt for foods. Accordingly, the child will spend his/her life thinking that the world owes him/her something. Such entitlement complex often comes with lofty expectations, for example, expectations that the world is a rational field where everyone cultivates ideas with logic and harvests rewards with reason; and expectations of the primacy of desire over handwork – meaning that life gives you whatever you desire, even when you don't work for it. Thus such expectations often come with a feeling of disappointment and regret. As typical of young people, when things do not happen as expected, which is often the case, they complain and do nothing, yet they expect things to change by themselves.

Indeed, I understand the logic that (most) older generations do not want to see their children go through the hardships they had gone through in their time. But, that's not a viable approach to adopt in raising a child to become self-reliant and self-sufficient. My stance is clear and it is that a child must be taught how to hunt for foods and not just be fed foods. Without any doubts, being fed foods and being taught how to hunt for foods have different outcomes on individuals. When you feed a child without teaching the child how to hunt for foods you are feeding the child's imagination that life is easy. Childhood is full of imaginations. At that stage we thought we could be anything and have everything that we wanted. As a child, I had lots of wild imaginations. I imagined I could be many things at the same time, for example, being the richest man on earth and at the same time a Roman Catholic

Priest – to become like Blessed Cyprian Iwene Tansi. Thus, it suffices to say that what a child is exposed to at an early age helps to shape both the child's childhood and adulthood. Therefore, when you are being fed you do not know what it means and takes to search for foods and get the foods ready. All you know is simply how to eat. So when you grow up with that mind-set, clearly you will think that the world is a bed of roses and that satisfying your needs and wants is a walk in the park. Eventually, when the realities of life begin to kick in and you begin to face all kinds of challenges from different sides you will be unable to sustain yourself.

However, on the contrary, if you are taught how to hunt for foods you will be exposed to avalanche of challenges that are associated with searching for foods, preparing the foods and even serving the foods. In essence, you will be exposed to all kinds of challenges and sufferings that come with them. What this means is that you will be better prepared to face whatever challenges that life confronts you with. As evident amongst young people across the world, a lot of the younger generations do not have the fortitude to deal with the challenges of life, simply because they have been fed for so long by their parents such that they do not have the prerequisite survival skills in the jungle – which is life. In my view, the failure of the older generations to teach their children how to hunt for foods is somehow responsible for many negative attitudes towards life that many of the younger generations display, so to speak. Because many of the younger generations have been fed foods without being taught how to hunt for foods they tend to be less inclined to take responsibilities for their actions, highly ignorant of the consequences of their actions, too complacent and lousy with anything, and less patient and easily pressured.